MW00624745

NUGGETS FROM NUMBERS

BIBLE STUDY AIDS *of William G. Heslop*

*Gems From Genesis
*Extras From Exodus
*Lessons From Leviticus
*Nuggets From Numbers
*Rubies From Ruth
*Sermon Seeds From The Psalms
*Pearls From the Poets and Prophets
*Diamonds From Daniel

NUGGETS FROM NUMBERS

Studies of Selected Portions from the
Book of Numbers

By
William G. Heslop, D.D., Litt., S.D.

KREGEL PUBLICATIONS
Grand Rapids, Michigan 49501

NUGGETS FROM NUMBERS copyright © 1958 by Higley Publishing Corporation, successors to original copyright owner, the Higley Printing Co. Reprinted in 1975 by Kregel Publications, a division of Kregel, Inc. under special arrangements with copyright owner. All rights reserved.

Library of Congress Catalog Card Number 75-13660
ISBN 0-8254-2828-9

First Edition 1958
Kregel Publications Edition 1975
Second Printing 1979

Printed in the United States of America

CONTENTS

FOREWORD

Nuggets from Numbers is the sequel to *Gems from Genesis, Extras from Exodus,* and *Lessons from Leviticus.* Speaking of Dr. Heslop's books, Reverend D. R. Raiser, of the Evangelical Reformed Church, stated, "I very much enjoyed the Heslop books. Dr. Heslop writes interestingly and fundamentally. I prefer him to many others whose books are widely heralded." A writer in the Moody Monthly, commenting upon one of Dr. Heslop's books, said, "Any book from the pen of this gifted author is always welcome. The lucidity, simplicity, and directness of style which characterize his writings, are found here also."

1

INTRODUCTION

Authorship of the Pentateuch

That Moses wrote the Pentateuch is plain to all who will follow their own feet.

1. "Moses was learned in all the wisdom of the Egyptians."
2. "Moses was mighty in words and deed."
3. "The Lord said unto Moses, Write . . . in a book."
4. "Moses wrote all the words of the Lord."
5. "And Moses wrote this law."
6. "As I was with Moses so will I be with thee."
7. "God made known his ways unto Moses."
8. "The law was given by Moses."
9. "Moses truly said . . . a prophet shall the Lord your God raise up . . . "
10. "Even unto this day, when Moses is read, the vail is upon their heart."
11. "Offer the gift that Moses commanded."
12. "Moses, because of the hardness of your hearts, suffered you to put away your wives."
13. "For Moses said, Honor thy father and thy mother."
14. "As Moses lifted up the serpent in the wilderness even *so*."

15. "Had ye believed Moses ye would have believed me, for he wrote of me."

Books of the Pentateuch

The key word of the Book of Genesis is *Beginning*:

1. Of the universe
2. Of the human race
3. Of human sin
4. Of redemption through sacrifice
5. Of family life
6. Of Godless civilization
7. Of Godless nations
8. Of languages
9. Of the Hebrew race
10. Of the Israelite race. (Including Jews)

The distinctive lessons of Genesis are:

1. The failure of man
2. The salvation of God
3. Where sin abounded, grace did much more abound.

As the oak is in the acorn, so every great leading truth is found in germ in the Book of Genesis.

In many respects it is the most important book in the Bible. Without it we would be ignorant as to the how of creation as well as ignorant of the first 1600 years of human history.

Dr. Adam Clarke has written "the narrative

is so simple, so much like truth, so consistent everywhere with itself, so correct in its dates, so impartial in its biography, so accurate in its philosophical details, so pure in its morality, so benevolent in its design, as amply to demonstrate that it never could have had an earthly origin."

The key word of the Book of Exodus is *Redemption:*

1. By power
2. By blood
3. By discipline
4. By obedience
5. By faith

Exodus is the sequel to Genesis. Genesis speaks of man's failure under every test, while Exodus shows us God meeting the failure of man by his divine grace, hastening to redeem, emancipate, and bless.

The book opens in gloom and ends in glory. At the beginning we find God coming down in grace to redeem and at the end we see God coming in glory to enrich by dwelling in their midst.

The keyword of the Book of Leviticus is *Worship,* and the key phrase is "Worship the Lord in the beauty of holiness."

The Hebrew title "Va-Yich-Rah" is very significant. It means "And he called." The Book sets forth God's call to access, communion, separation, holiness of spirit, soul and body, and holy worship in his holy presence.

Since it embraces the history of one month only, it may justly lay claim to the most remarkable book in the Old Testament.

While studying this wonderful book I was impressed by the absence of any mention, in any way, of the Holy Spirit. The Holy Spirit is not once named. *He* seems to have been so preeminently occupied in his work of glorifying Christ that everything in the Book relates to the second person of the adorable trinity.

The outline of Leviticus is:

1. Worship as the result of sacrifice
2. Worship through a Mediator
3. Worship the Lord in the beauty of holiness

The key words of the Book of Numbers are *walk* and *warfare.*

The book of Numbers sets forth the walk and warfare of the believer.

The distinctive lessons are:

1. The faithfulness of God
2. The failure of man
3. God's provision for man's failure

In Genesis, Israel is chosen to be the peculiar people of God. In Exodus, they are redeeemed. In Leviticus, they draw near to God in worship, communion and holiness. In Numbers, they are called to conquest as warriors in the name of the Lord.

In Genesis man is *ruined* by sin. In Exodus man is *redeemed by blood.* In Leviticus redeemed man is found worshipping the Lord in the beauty of holiness. In Numbers redeemed and worshipping man is found walking and warring for Jehovah.

In Genesis Israel is in the loins of Abraham. In Exodus Israel is in the brick kilns. In Leviticus Israel is around the tabernacle. In Numbers Israel is in the wilderness.

In Genesis we have Israel's election. In Exodus we have Israel's redemption. In Leviticus we have Israel's worship. In Numbers we have Israel's walk and warfare.

Facts about Numbers

I. The Name

The book of Numbers derives its name from the fact that it records the enumeration of Israel. Numbers is also the book of the "Journeyings" since it gives an account of Israel's wilderness journeyings from Sinai to Moab.

II. The Writer

Moses was the human writer inspired by the Spirit to pen these wonderful words.

III. The Date

The Book of Numbers was written about 1500 B.C.

IV. Divisions

Numbers has three great divisions.

1. The faithfulness of God
2. The failure of man
3. God's provision for man's failure

Brief Outline of the Book of Numbers

I. The Faithfulness of God

1. Preparation for War
2. Sanctification of the Camp
3. Divine Guidance
   (1) Moses (Type of Christ)
   (2) Pillar of Fire (Type of the Holy Spirit)
   (3) The Trumpets (Type of the Word)
   (Christ, the Holy Spirit, and the Word assure the saints of divine guidance.)

The faithfulness of God is clearly seen in the fact that 3,000,000 men, women, and children enter into, and pass through, a sterile desert without a drop of water, loaf of bread, or blade of grass. Selah! An army of 3,000,000 men, women, and children enter into and pass through a trackless, pathless, uncharted desert without a guide, compass, chart, map, footstep, finger post, or stop and go sign. A city equal in size to the city of Chicago without a grocery store, bakery, meat market, surgeon, doctor, butcher, undertaker, candlestick maker, drug store, or hospital. Selah! Think of the faithfulness of God.

II. The Failure of man

1. Israel failed
   (1) At Marah
   (2) At Taberah
   (3) At Kibroth-hattaavah
   (4) At Ai

2. Moses failed
   (1) Slew the Egyptian
   (2) Asked for Aaron
   (3) Requested Hobab's presence
   (4) Jethro
   (5) Smote the rock twice

3. Joshua failed
   (1) Case of Eldad and Medad
   (2) Defeat at Ai
   (3) Blamed God

4. Miriam failed
   (1) Gossiped about Moses
   (2) Leprosy

5. Aaron failed
   (1) Listened to Miriam
   (2) Made golden calf

6. The spies failed
   (1) First determined to spy the land
   (2) Discouraged the people
   (3) Refused to go over

7. Korah failed

    (1) Rebelled
    (2) Slandered Moses
    (3) Coveted position and power

8. The great refusal and failure at Kadesh-barnea

III. God's Provision for Man's failure

1. The red heifer
2. The brazen serpent
3. The cities of refuge
4. The rod of Aaron
5. The Priests and Levites

The faithfulness and patience of God is the supreme revelation of the book of Numbers.

A Geographical Division of the Book of Numbers

Chapters

I. At Sinai 1-10

(1) Number of the Tribes
(2) Order of the Tribes
(3) The Duties of the Levites

II. From Sinai to Kadesh 11-19

(1) Seventy Elders Chosen
(2) The Twelve Spies
(3) The Rebellion of Korah
(4) The Red Heifer and Water of Separation

III. From Kadesh to Moab 20-36

(1) The Death of Miriam
(2) The Rock Smitten
(3) The Plague of Serpents
(4) Balaam and Balak
(5) The Appointment of Joshua

2

FIGHT THE GOOD FIGHT OF FAITH

(Numbers 1:1-4)

1. And the LORD spake unto Moses in the wilderness of Sinai, in the tabernacle of the congregation, on the first day of the second month, in the second year after they were come out of the land of Egypt, saying,

2. Take ye the sum of all the congregation of the children of Israel, after their families, by the house of their fathers, with the number of their names, every male by their polls;

3. From twenty years old and upward, all that are able to go forth to war in Israel: thou and Aaron shall number them by their armies.

4. And with you there shall be a man of every tribe; every one head of the house of his fathers.

1. *Our names are in the Book of Life.* God has his people both numbered and named.

God told Ananias that a man named *Saul* was in the house of Simon, who lived in a street called *Strait.*

God called the boy Samuel by name saying, *"Samuel, Samuel,"* for "he calleth his own sheep by name."

When the glorified Christ appeared to Saul of Tarsus, he said unto him, "Saul, Saul, why?"

Christ mentioned the sister of Mary and Lazarus by name, saying, "Martha, Martha, thou art careful and troubled about many things: But!"

At the grave of their dead brother, Christ called by name saying, "*Lazarus*, come forth."

After the resurrection, Christ said, "Go tell my disciples and Peter." Peter's heart was broken, and, disgusted with himself and thoroughly ashamed, he needed a special message of consolation, cheer, and hope. A general invitation was not sufficient, and hence it is written, "my disciples and Peter."

God knows where we live and knows our names, and even a Rahab may have her name in the book of life side by side with a Moses and a Joseph.

2. *Having been redeemed in Exodus and brought nigh to God in Leviticus, Israel must now learn to fight.* Israel must now learn to war a good warfare. They must now learn to walk instead of being carried. They must now learn to fight instead of being nursed and entertained. They must learn to keep rank, to be in subjection, and to obey. They must learn that mere trifles such as cold, snow, heat and rain, while tremendous hindrances to babes, are not to be allowed to stop soldiers. War. "All that are able to go forth to war."

Having been redeemed by the blood of the passover lamb, they must now be prepared for war.

"The fight is on, Oh Christian soldier!
And face to face in stern array;
With armour gleaming and banner streaming,
The right and wrong engage today.
The fight is on! but be not weary,
Be strong and in his might hold fast:
If God be for us, His banner o'er us,
We'll sing the victor's song at last."

3. *They must declare their pedigree.* They must give testimony as to when and where they were born. Warriors must know when and where they were born again and give clear testimony and proof of the same. I *hope* I am saved, or I *think* I am saved, is not sufficient. We must *know* we are saved. This is more than church membership or water baptism. We *know* whom we have believed. We *know* we have passed from death unto life. One thing I *know*.

4. *Israel must have a standard.* They must march either under Judah, Reuben, Ephraim, or Dan. They must know when and where they were born, they must prove by their pedigree that they are the people of God. They must keep separated from others and must be ready to endure hardness, keep rank, be submissive and obedient.

What was necessary for Israel is necessary for us if we would war a good warfare. We too must have a standard. We too, by our pedigree, must be able to prove that we are the people of God. We too must keep separated from that which is unholy and unclean. We must be ready to endure hardness as good soldiers of Jesus Christ. We must be submissive and obedient and keep rank if we would win in this warfare.

1. Must be born again
2. Must know (assurance) that we are the people of God
3. Keep separated
4. Endure hardness
5. Be submissive and obedient

Here are some simple essentials in order to war a good warfare.

3

MEN OF WAR

(Numbers 1:1-16)

Men. Men of War. Men of Renown. Not men of riches, but men of renown. Not men out for peace at any price, but men of war. *Men.* Transformed men. Regenerated men. Holy Ghost filled men. Men, changed from fugitives to fighters, transformed from slaves to soldiers, and from weaklings to warriors. *All* men of war, changed from craving cowards to sanctified saints and praying soldiers too.

The people of God were to become a powerful army. They were to go forth and fight. They were not ordered to erect a nursery, or establish an entertainment bureau, or set up a popsicle stand. God's saints were to be soldiers and not babies.

Let us look at the names of the men who were to be heads, princes, the renowned of the congregation. First we have the tribe of Reuben and with him there was Elizur the son of Shedeur.

Reuben means, *behold a son.*

When Reuben was born the mother said, "Look, I have received a son," and she called his name Reuben.

The Hebrew word Ben means "A Son" and

Reu means "look." Behold a son. Sonship is the first necessity in order to be a good soldier of Christ. We must be born again before we can fight the good fight. Have you been born from above? Reuben could declare his pedigree. He knew where and when he was born.

Do you know where and when you were born again? If not, you cannot win in this warfare. Stand aside. Step back. You cannot be a soldier in the army of God.

With Reuben was Elizur.

Elizur means, *God is my strength.*

Strength is necessary in time of war. Instead of fussing and faultfinding, we are going to fight the good fight and for this, God is our strength. Side by side and shoulder to shoulder we stand and do battle in the name of God our strength. The strength and the support of a just and holy God will save you from the jim-jams and jitters. The strength of God will stiffen your spine. When God is with you to strengthen you, you can whip your weight in wild cats and chase a thousand devils. Hallelujah!

Again notice, that Elizur was the son of Shedeur. The word *Shedeur* means fiery, to be on fire. No wonder they were in the front of the fight, and leaders in the conflict.

Born again ones, with God as their strength and on fire with a holy zeal for God and his cause, who or what could stop such soldiers? The crying need of the hour is for men of fire. We have plenty of machinery, we have almost perfect organization, and we have ample funds, but where are the men of fire? Mighty men like Moses. Courageous men like Caleb. Just and fearless men like Joshua. Pure and unselfish men like Paul. Winsome and scholarly men like Wesley. Big men with holy hearts like Booth and Bresee. God give us men, men of fire, men of zeal, men of flinty faces and clenched fists, who will go up to war against the mighty.

After the tribe of Reuben, the tribe of Simeon was chosen, and with the tribe of Simeon was Shelumiel, the son of Zuri-shaddai. The word Simeon means *to hearken.* When Simeon was born, the mother said that the Lord had hearkened to her cry and hence she called his name Simeon.

If there were more tears, more heart cries to God from mothers, there would be more answers from a giving God. If more mothers would hearken to God and go God's way, there would be much less wilfulness, waywardness, and wickedness in our weary world. It pays to listen to God. We had better hearken to the voice of the Lord. To be good soldiers, it is imperative that we obey God. Listen to God and obey his Word.

With Simeon was Shelumiel, which means *the friend of God.* No one should despise friendships. We have a small picture in our home with the undying words of a forgotten man whose name was Sam W. Foss. The words read thus:

"Let me live in a house
by the side of the road
And be a friend of man."

I think it was Van Dyke who wrote:

"The lintel low enough to keep out pomp and pride;
The threshold high enough to turn deceit aside;
The door band strong enough from robbers to defend;
This door will open at a touch to welcome every friend."

Of all friends, the best friend is GOD, and without God, the most popular persons are friendless. Let us ask God to be our friend and let us so live that God will welcome our friendship.

Zuri- Shaddai means, *The rock of the Almighty.* The word Zuri means rock and Shaddai means all sufficient.

In the home, in business, in church and on the street, God is all sufficient. There is not a problem that he cannot solve. There is not a question that he cannot answer. There is not a need that he cannot supply. There is not a sin that he cannot forgive or an emergency that he does not understand. He is the Almighty, the All-sufficient One. He is all-sufficient in every circumstance and in every situation. He is sufficient for you, sufficient for your home, sufficient for your business, sufficient for your body and for your brain. He is sufficient for your soul, for all time and all eternity. He is sufficient in life, and will be sufficient as we approach the last mile of the way and come face to face with the last enemy, which is death.

The next tribe was the tribe of Judah, and with him was Nahshon the son of Anninadab.

The word *Judah* means *praise*. When Judah was born, the happy mother began to shout the praises of God and called his name Judah, which means praise. To be well prepared for war we must be born again (Reuben); strengthened by God, (Elizur); keep a hot heart (Shedeur); listen to God (Simeon); make God our constant friend (Shelumiel); and rely on our sufficient captain (Zurishaddai); and learn to shout and praise God (Judah).

Praise God that we are alive. Praise God for food to eat and clothes to wear. Praise God for water to drink and homes in which we may live. Praise God for the measure of health of body and strength of mind which are ours. Praise God that we are on the outside of a hospital for the sick and an asylum for the insane. Praise God that we are out of the cemetery and out of hell. Hallelujah. Praise God that our sins are all forgiven and that our hearts are purified. You say that you do not believe in shouting. There's a reason. Some of you are so cold, so dead, so luke warm that you do not have fire enough to generate sufficient steam even to whistle. Some of you have been so crooked and so loose in your ways and so glib with your tongue, you would not dare to shout. There are those present who know you too well. Some of you have forgivenesses to ask, wrongs to make right, confessions to make, back-slidings to acknowledge, and sins to be pardoned. Of course *you* do not believe in shouting the praises of God. Forget your dignity and self-importance and jump for joy. Put away your polished, pretty refineries and praise God before the potter's field gets your poor body.

Perhaps your wife has a different explanation for your not praising God. How about that?

Oh! brother, sister, learn to praise God. Make wrongs right as far as you can, and start praising God. Do not let anything in the past stop you from praising God in the present. Let the grumblers grumble, and the grunters grunt, but we must praise God. He is so good and so kind and so patient and so gentle. Praise God. He is worthy of all our praises, therefore, praise the Lord!

With Judah was Nahshon, the son of Amminadab.

The word *Nahshon* means *spell.* The word means *to bubble over,* to have a spell in a good sense, to have a religious spell.

Most people are subject to spells in the wrong way. Feelings get hurt, friends visit others but not you, some one else is appointed Sunday school superintendent or janitor, and you have a spell and go around with the blues or the greens. Others are asked to lead prayer meetings, play the piano, and sing in the choir, and you are neglected. You are not even invited to stew the oysters. You poor baby. Then there are others who have a spell in a good sense. He was a good soldier of Jehovah. He saw the enemy but he also saw God. And seeing God he had an old fashioned Methodist, evangelical, Nazarene spell. He became jumping happy because God was with his people. Amminadab means *the people of liberality.*

The word Nadab means liberal, generous, and the word Ammi means people. God's people are a liberal people. It is easy for them to open their purse strings and give to God and to God's cause. Unsparingly, ungrudgingly, and unstintingly they give of their means for missions at home and abroad.

A stingy, close-fisted pinch-penny is a misery to himself and all mankind. Such are useless in peace or war, but in war they are a positive hindrance. Think of an army composed of men who have been born from above, and have the strength of God, and the sufficiency of God the Almighty, and liberal and lavish for the cause of God and holiness! This poor, sin-blighted, sin-blasted, bruised and bleeding, broken hearted world is in need of Christ and full salvation. Christ is the only remedy for the world's ruin. Christ is the only hope for the world's woe. Oh, for a liberal people who will give the gospel to the ends of the earth.

Next to the tribe of Judah came Issachar and with Issachar there was Nethaneel, the son of Zuar.

The word *Issachar* means *to hire.*

"Now hath the Lord granted me my hire," said the happy mother, and she called him Issachar.

The picture is that of a harvest field waving with golden grain and of reapers being hired to garner the grain.

The fields are white to harvest but the labourers are few.

The word *Nethaneel* means *given of God,* while *Zuar* means *very small.* I think that we might receive profitable instruction from these names.

Every good gift, however small it may seem, cometh down from above, and we thank God that he takes the little things, and small, insignificant people to help him in the war against sin and Satan. Side by side with the man on fire and the man with the strength of God and the sufficiency of God is the one who is very small (Zuar). They were one host and one army and with Jehovah as their captain they whipped all their enemies.

Some of you may be very small and not be able to do very much, but are you doing that which is possible? Are you giving our tithes and giving as God has prospered you? Your little, added to some one else's little, may mean much to the cause of Christ and holiness. Your light, placed side by side with other lights, may help guide someone to glory. What do you say if we make up our minds to keep in step with the whole army—and, side by side and shoulder to shoulder—support the whole program of Christ and the Church?

The tribe of Zebulon followed the tribe of Issachar and with him was Eliab the son of Helon.

The word *Zebulon* means to *abide*.

"Abide in me," said Jesus. It is not only necessary to obtain the blessing but it is important to maintain it, keep it, abide. Endure, go on, be persistent, stand fast, continue in the faith, *Abide*. The word *Eliab* means *"God is my Father."* Think of going to war with the consciousness that the God of gods, the God of the earth and the heavens is *your Father*. What strength and courage must come to the tired servant and courier of God to realize that God is his father.

"Your Father knoweth."

The word *Helon* means *very strong*.

Side by side and shoulder to shoulder, these believing, fearless soldiers fought the battles of Jehovah.

"Be thou strong and very courageous."

"Be strong in the Lord."

"The joy of the Lord is your strength."

"The people who do know their God shall be strong and do exploits."

All these names in Numbers have a meaning for us today. When the fight is on, you need a Judah who can praise the Lord. You need an Elizur and a Helon in the battle against sin and hell. In the strife and struggle against sin and Satan there is need of a Shelumiel and a Nethaneel.

Amid the clash of arms, the tussle, the conflict and the collision of spirit forces, one needs a Nahshon who can have a spell and give the devil a cataleptic fit.

If there is to be the needed endurance in this fight of faith, there must be the Eliabs who never lose sight of the truth that God is Father and Friend.

This scribe had a wonderful opportunity to make some money this week. Two business men waited upon me and offered me a coffee and doughnut stand in the middle of our busy main avenue in our business section. They wanted the president of the W.F.M.S. to be in charge. Imagine an elect lady like Mrs. Henry Geukes, the honored president of our great Missionary Society selling hot dogs, hamburgers, and coffee for ten cents and shouting glory to God, hallelujah, come and get your hot dog. They must not realize that we are enjoying something better than hot dogs and coffee.

Imagine our good friends here, Alma and Lois Pratt, in the middle of the highway spreading mustard on a hamburger instead of seeking to put a blister on the devil. They invited me, too, to be the judge of what turned out to be the nudist colony.

God pity our ministers, and maidens of our churches who sell their birthright for a soup stand on the street to help poor Jesus to carry on his sacred cause.

We certainly need some Judahs (praise) and Nashons (spells). But to continue the interesting list of princes and renowned leaders in the army of the Lord.

After Zebulon came Ephraim and with him there was Elishama the son of Ammihud.

Ephraim was the son of Joseph.

The word *Joseph* means *to add, to increase,* while the name *Ephraim* means *to be fruitful.*

With Ephraim was *Elishama,* whose name means *God of my ears.* He was the son of *Ammihud,* which means *the people of majesty.*

How fortunate to have such fighters in the battle royal against the bewitching, bewildering attacks of the world, the flesh and the devil. In this pitched battle against the forces of impurity and unholiness, how encouraging to know that we may add to our faith, virtue, etc. How comforting to know that our ears are attuned to heaven and God and that we are a part of the people of God, the people of majesty. In this spiritual Armageddon we need the Ephraims to bring forth fruit unto holiness, the Elishmas, whose ears are in tune with the Infinite, and the Ammihuds who are conscious of their high calling, *the people of majesty.*

Next in order was the tribe of Manasseh and with him was Gamaliel, the son of Pedahzur.

The word *Manasseh* means *to forget.*

"Forgetting those things which are behind."

Forget the failures, the mistakes, the side steps of the past, and press on in the present with hope, and confidence in the future. Forget the insults and the neglects, also the imaginary insults and neglects, and forget the victories of the past too, for we cannot win the war today by boasting of our victories of yesterday. If some one has slighted you, injured you, mistreated you, misjudged you, forget it and fight on.

Hard knocks are helps to holiness. Do not allow bones of contention in your ranks to weaken the army and help the enemy. Forget. Forget it. In this fisticuffs against false doctrines and false beliefs on every hand, let us insist on friendliness within our own four walls. In our scrap against sin let us refuse to step aside by scrapping among ourselves.

In this tremendous tussle against the increasing tide of worldliness, want and woe, let us be true to God and true to each other. What say you?

In grappling with the forces of greed and godlessness without, let us not be fussing within. Learn to forget. Be a faithful Manasseh-ite and *forget.* Forgive and forget.

The word *Gamaliel* means *God will recompense.*

The struggle may be hard, long and severe, but God will see to the recompense of reward.

In God's name, let's come to blows with unbelief and backsliding, relying on the God of recompense.

Let us try conclusions with conceit and carnality, depending on God who has promised and is able to perform.

Let's measure swords and exchange shots against all the onslaughts of Satan, and in God's name we shall succeed.

Let's take up the cudgels against all carnality, and with a cleansed heart and consecrated hands and lips, contend earnestly for the faith, and God himself will be our present recompense and future reward. The word Peduhzur means *redeemed by power.*

The Israelites were redeemed by (1) love (2) power (3) blood. All redemption is by love, power, and blood. In this grim visaged war against sickness, wilfulness, and worldliness, we need and we have the presence and the power of God at our disposal.

In our campaign against crookedness and carnality, both in city and in country, we are not left to our own resources.

Worldly strategy can never win in the war against sin and Satan. Nothing less than the presence and power of an all sufficient Saviour can overcome the forces of sin and self in our world today.

We need the power of the Pedahzurs, the grace of the Gamaliels and the forgiving and the forgetting love of the Manassehs.

And so we might continue, for we need the

Benjamins (sons of sorrow) and the Gideons (cutter down).

We also need Dan (to judge), Ahiezer (brother of help), Ammi-shaddai (people of the Almighty), Asher (happy), Gad (to overcome), and Naphtali (to wrestle). All are needed in the battle against unrighteousness and unholiness.

To arms! To your tents, oh Israel! In the thick of the fray let us fight together in this good fight of faith.

With the sword (Bible) in hand, let us hopefully meet the embattled hosts of hell. Let us cut our way through, and over the top, for Jesus let us go hand in hand, side by side and shoulder to shoulder, with our holiness banner unfurled, assured of final triumph in the name of our God.

Holiness shall yet ascend the throne and sin be placed upon the scaffold. Hallelujah, Amen.

4

THE LEVITES

(Numbers 1:47-54)

1. Separated Ministry

   God's people have always been a separated people. Abraham, Israel, the Church of Christ, and the Bride of Christ were and are a separated and peculiar people.

2. Holy Ministry

   God is a holy God and cannot tolerate an unholy ministry, walk, or warfare.

3. Chosen by Sovereign Grace

   The Levites were not one whit better than any one of the other thousands of Israel. Grace and grace alone met their need. As God called Abram out of Ur of the Chaldees and Israel out of Egypt, so he called the sons of Levi to be his ministers.

4. Commissioned by God

   God called them out and separated them.
   God called them in and sanctified them.
   God sent them forth and empowered them.

5. Given to Aaron

   As Aaron was a type of Christ so the Levites were a type of believers, ministers who war a good warfare in the fight against sin.

6. Peculiarly the Lord's

   God is no respecter of persons, but he is a respecter of character and calling. Israel was peculiarly the Lord's, and the Levites were peculiarly the Lord's, and God's ministers today are peculiarly the Lord's. "Touch not mine anointed."

7. Charge of the Tabernacle

   They carried the sacred Tabernacle with its sacred furnishings. The Tabernacle was a type of Christ. It is the happy calling of ministers as it is their blessed privilege to have Christ in them and make him known to the world.

8. Mediators as Well as ministers

   To intercede for others is a high honor. To stand in the gap between the living and the dead may be a prize to be coveted by the angelic hosts. New Testament ministers are mediators. They bring God and man together. Peace is made, righteousness and mercy kiss each other, and homes and hearts are thereby made happy.

9. Custodians of the Lord's Treasures

   What treasure in earthen vessels!—pardon, peace, purity, and power. This also reminds us of our stewardship. The Levites were stewards, keepers, custodians—Stewardship of time, money, life, and influence. God must be Lord of all or he is *not* Lord at all.

10. Three Classes of Levites

    (1) Kohathites (Sons of Kohath)
    (2) Gershomites (Sons of Gershom)
    (3) Merarites (Sons of Merari)

    These three classes correspond to the New Testament pastors, evangelists, and teachers. God has a place for all and a plan for all. He has a work for every worker, and every man has his work.

The following notes clearly set forth the beautiful harmony between the Old Testament and the New.

1. *"The Levites shall be mine"* (Num. 8:14).

   "They are thine; all mine are thine and thine are mine" (John 17:9-10).

2. *"They are wholly given unto me; them have I taken unto me"* (Num. 8:16).

   "To take out of them a people for his name" (Acts 15:14).

3. *"I have taken the Levites instead of the first-born"* (Num. 3:12).

   "The church of the first born which are written in heaven" (Heb. 12:23)

4. *"The Lord thy God hath chosen him out of all thy tribes"* (Deut. 18:5).

   "I have chosen you out of the world" (John 15:19).

5. *"The Lord hath chosen you to minister and to bless"* (Deut. 21:5).

   "Ye are a chosen generation that ye should shew forth the praises of him . . . ."(I Peter 2:9)

6. *"Chosen to carry the ark"* (I Chron. 15:2).

   "Chosen to bear my name before the Gentiles" (Acts 9:15).

7. *"The Levites were expressed by name"* (I Chron. 16:41).

   "He calleth his own sheep by name" (John 10:3).

8. *"Bring the tribe of Levi near"* (Num. 3:5-6).

   "Made nigh by the blood of Christ" (Eph. 2:13).

9. *"That they may be joined unto thee"* (Num. 18:2)

   "He that is joined unto the Lord is one spirit" (I Cor. 6:17).

10. *"I have given the Levites to Aaron"* (Num. 8:19).

    "Thou gavest them me" (Christ) (John 17:6).

11. *"Thou shalt anoint them"* (Exodus 40:15).

    "Ye have an unction from the holy one" (I John 2:20).

12. *"I will sanctify them"* (Exodus 29:44).
    "Sanctify them" (John 17:17).

13. *"The Priest's lips shall keep knowledge"* (Mal. 2:7).
    "Filled with all knowledge" (Rom. 15:14).

14. *"The Levites were upright in heart"* (II Chron. 29:34).
    "Blessed are the pure in heart" (Matt. 5:8).

15. *"The Levites were able men"* (I Chron. 26:8).
    "Able ministers of the New Testament" (II Cor. 3:6).

16. *"The Levites were able men for strength"* (I Chron. 26:8).
    "Be strong in the Lord" (Eph. 6:10).

17. *"Thou shalt separate the Levites"* (Num. 8:14).
    "Come out from among them and be ye separate" (II Cor. 6:17).

18. *"Do not drink wine nor strong drink lest ye die"* (Lev. 10:8-9).
    "Be not drunk with wine but be filled with the Spirit" (Eph. 5:18).

19. *"Take the Levites and cleanse them"* (Num. 8:6-7).
    "Let us cleanse ourselves from all filthiness of the flesh and spirit" (II Cor. 7:1).

20. *"And the Levites were purified"* (Num. 8:21).
"That he might purify unto himself a peculiar people" (Titus 2:14).

21. *"And thou shalt put coats upon them"* (Exodus 29:8).
"Put ye on the Lord Jesus Christ" (Rom. 13:14).
"Put on charity" (Col. 3:12-14).

22. *"Thou shalt gird them with girdles"* (Exod. 29:9).
"Stand therefore having your loins girt about with truth" (Eph. 6:14).

23. *"Let thy priests be clothed with righteousness"* (Psalms 132:9).
"Having on the breastplate of righteousness" (Eph. 6:14).

24. *"Sanctify them"* (Exod. 28:41).
"Sanctify them" (John 17:17).
"The God of peace sanctify you wholly" (I Thess. 5:23).

25. *"After that . . . service"* (Numbers 8:22).
"Being then made free from sin ye became servants" (Rom. 6:18).

26. *"Shall be satisfied"* (Jer. 31:14).
"I am the bread of life" (John 6:35).

27. *"A certain portion . . . due for each day"* (Neh. 11:23).

    "Give us day by day our daily bread" (Luke 11:3).

28. *"And they departed not from the king's commandments"* (II Chron. 8:15; 35:10).

    "Ye are my friends if ye do whatsoever I command you" (John 15:14).

29. *"They were employed day and night"* (I Chron 9:33).

    "Always abounding in the work of the Lord" (I Cor. 15:58).

30. *"And the porters waited"* (II Chron. 35:15).

    "Blessed is that servant whom his Lord when he cometh shall find so doing" (Matt. 24:46).

5

POWER OF LITTLE THINGS

(Numbers 4:1-29)

Tiny snow flakes may block the busiest highway and defy the stoutest plows. Drops of water may sweep away a city, making thousands homeless. Insects may leave a whole state devoid of a blade of grass or a single green leaf. A tiny worm may despoil the most beautiful trees. Tuberculosis germs may slowly weaken the pillars which carry the strongest and healthiest looking man in town and in a few short weeks drag him to the cemetery. The giant redwoods of California were once small seeds. *The pins and cords* of the tabernacle were very important little things. They were necessary to the perfection and harmony of the whole. A good symphony baton waver will quickly miss the notes of even the piccolo. Those who attended to the pins and cords of God's house, like the player of the piccolo in an orchestra, rendered useful and essential service. Willing workers and helpers in the smallest matters will share alike in the day of rewards. Those who refuse to help at all because they cannot do some big thing or take the leading part injure themselves as well as the cause of Christ. The least and lowliest service given to God shall be everlastingly and gratefully remembered in the day of the giving of crowns.

"It is little;
But in these sharp extremities of fortune,
The blessings which the weak and poor can scatter
Have their own season.
It is a little thing to speak a phrase
Of common comfort, which by daily use
Has almost lost its sense; yet on the ear
Of him who thought to die unmourn'd 'twill fall
Like choicest music: fill the glazing eye
With gentle tears; relax the knotted hand;
To know the bonds of fellowship again;
And shed on the departing soul a sense
More precious than the benison of friends.
About the honor'd death-bed of the rich,
To him who else were lonely, that another
Of the great family is near and feels."—Talfourd

"Do little things as if they were great, because of the majesty of the Lord Jesus Christ, who dwells in thee; and do great things as if they were little and easy, because of His omnipotence."—Pascal

"The most ordinary and unimportant actions of a man's life will often show more of his natural character and his habits than more important actions, which are done deliberately, and sometimes against his natural inclinations."—Abp. Whately

"Says a quaint but forcible author, there is not a man or a thing now alive, but has tools to work with. The basest of created animalcules, the spider itself, has a spinning jenny and warping mill and power looms within its head: the stupidest of oysters has a Pepin's digester with a limestone house to hold it in."—E. L. Magoon

Illustrations

(a) "Where God in generous fulness dwells,
Nor small nor great is known;
He paints the tiniest floweret-cells
O'er emerald meadows strewn;
And sees, but not with kinder eyes,
The heavens grow rich with sunset dyes;
Both ministrant to beauty's sense,
Both signs of one Omnipotence.

He comes not forth with pageant grand
His marvels to perform.
A cloud "the bigness of a hand"
Can blacken heaven with a storm.
A grain of dust, if he arrange,
The fortunes of a planet change.
An insect reef can overwhelm
The stately navies of a realm.

There are no trifles. Arks as frail
As bore God's prince of old,
On many a buoyant Nile stream sail
The age's heirs to hold.
From Jacob's love on Joseph shed,
Came Egypt's wealth and Israel's bread;

From Ruth's chance gleaning in the corn,
The Psalmist sang—the Christ was born."
W. M. Punshon

(b) "Have you ever watched an icicle as it formed? You noticed how it froze one drop at a time, until it was a foot long or more. If the water was clear, the icicle remained clear, and sparkled brightly in the sun; but if the water was but slightly muddy, the icicle looked foul, and its beauty was spoiled. Just so our characters are forming: one little thought or feeling at a time adds its influence. If each thought be pure and right, the soul will be lovely, and sparkle with happiness; but if impure and wrong, there will be deformity and wretchedness."—Temperance Anecdotes, in Dictionary of Illustrations.

(c) "Little things are seeds of great ones. Little cruelties are gems of great ones. Little treacheries are, like small holes in raiment, the beginning of large ones. Little dishonesties are like the drops that work through the bank of the river; a drop is an engineer: it tunnels a way for its fellows, and they, rushing, prepare for all behind them. A worm in a ship's plank proves, in time, worse than a cannon-ball." H. W. Beecher

(d) "Let us be content to work,
To do the thing we can, and not presume
To fret because it's little. 'Twill employ
Seven men, they say, to make a perfect pin.

Who makes the head consents to miss the
    point;
Who makes the point agrees to leave the
    head;
And if a man should cry, 'I want a pin,
And I must make it straightway, head and
    point,'
His wisdom is not worth the pin he wants."
—Elizabeth B. Browning

6

CLEANSING, SANCTIFICATION

(Numbers 5:1-4)

1. And the Lord spake unto Moses, saying,
2. Command the children of Israel, that they put out of the camp every leper, and every one that hath an issue, and whosoever is defiled by the dead.
3. Both male and female shall ye put out, without the camp shall ye put them, that they defile not their camps, in the midst whereof I dwell.
4. And the children of Israel did so, and put them out without the camp: as the LORD spake unto Moses, so did the children of Israel.

1. The Leper (Sin Working Within)

God is represented as being in the midst of his people. The God who flung flaming worlds into space, who scooped out the oceans, piled up the mountains and carpeted the earth with green, and whom the heavens cannot contain, has nevertheless condescended to dwell in the midst of his purified and obedient people. The God of the Old and the Emmanuel of the New Testament is with us. With us in the home, with us in business, and with us on the street. His remaining with us however is conditional.

(1) "Put out every leper."
Leprosy is the Bible type of sin working within. It is the plague of the heart and is uncleanness. God cannot and will not stay in the midst of encouraged unholiness.

(2) "The children of Israel did so."
An obedient people is God's delight. Parents delight in the obedience of a child.

2. An Issue (Sin Working Without)
"Put out every one that hath an issue."
The clean must be kept separate from the unclean. An issue is proof of something radically wrong within. Nothing foul, festering, impure, unclean, or polluting was permitted in the camp in the midst of which God desired to dwell.

3. Defilement of the Dead
"Put out whosoever is defiled by the dead."
It is possible to mix with unsaved and unholy relatives and friends so long that defilement and contamination result. One rotten apple will soon turn a barrel of good apples into corruption. We become like those with whom we associate. God will not stay where there is encouraged, or permitted sin and uncleanness. He cannot bless unholiness.

Illustrations

(a) "Cleanliness may be defined to be the emblem of purity of mind, and may be recommended under the three following heads; as it is a mark of politeness, as it produces affection, and as it bears analogy to chastity of sentiment. First, it is a mark of politeness, for it is universally agreed upon, that no one unadorned with this virtue can go into company without giving a manifold offence; the different nations of the world as much distinguished by their cleanliness as by their arts and sciences; the more they are advanced in civilization the more they consult this part of politeness. Secondly, cleanliness may be said to be the foster-mother of affection. Beauty commonly produces love, but cleanliness preserves it. Age itself is not unamiable while it is preserved clean and unsullied; like a piece of metal constantly kept smooth and bright, we look on it with more pleasure than on a new vessel cankered with rust. I might further observe, that as cleanliness renders us agreeable to others, it makes us easy to ourselves, that it is an excellent preservative of health; and that several vices, both of mind and body, are inconsistent with the habit of it. In the third place, it bears a great analogy with chastity of sentiment, and naturally inspires refined feelings and passions; we find from experience, that through the prevalence of custom, the most vicious actions lose their horror by being made familiar to us. On the contrary, those who live in the neighbourhood of good examples fly from the first appearance of what is shocking; and thus pure and unsullied thoughts are naturally suggested to the mind by those objects that perpetually encompass us when they are beautiful and elegant in their kind."—Addison

"It is wonderful how views of life depend upon exercise and right management of the physical constitution. Nor is this, rightly looked at, any cause for perplexity, though it seems so at first; for though you might be inclined to view it as a degradation of our higher nature to find it so dependent on the lower, and hope and faith and energy resultant from a walk or early hours—yet, in fact, it is only a proof that all the laws of our manifold being are sacred, and that disobedience to them is punished by God. And the punishment in one department of our nature of the transgressions committed in the other—as, for instance, when mental gloom comes from uncleanliness or physical inertia, and, on the other hand, where ill-health ensues from envy or protracted doubt—is but one of many instances of the law of vicarious suffering. We are, as it were, two, and one suffers by what the other does." —F. W. Robertson, M.A., Life and Letters

(b) "They are deceived that think it is not necessary to purge out the great and gross offenders. The Church is the City of God, excommunication is the sword; it is the school of Christ, this is the rod, as the Apostle calleth it; it is the Temple of God, this is, as it were, the whip, to scourge out such as abuse it and themselves; it is the body of Christ, this is as a medicine to cure the diseases of it; it is the vine and sheepfold, this serveth to keep the foxes and wolves from it."—W. Attersoll

(c) "How real is that description of sin—'it defileth, it worketh abomination, it maketh a lie!' It is uncleanness, unloveliness, untruth! But it shall 'in no wise enter' heaven. There 'shall be nothing to hurt and to destroy.' Moral evil cannot for a moment dwell in it. As though the leprosy of sin had struck too inextricably into the abode of man, had even contaminated the habitation of angels, we anticipate a scene purer than earth could afford however it were changed, purer than the heavens from which the angels fell. And when we can conceive of such a state, that which gives to law all its power of sway and yet debars its curse, that is heaven, the highest heaven, the heaven of heavens! We know it by this, we desire it for this, 'wherein dwelleth righteousness!' "—R. W. Hamilton, LL.D., D.D.

7

THE SPIRIT OF JEALOUSY

(Numbers 5:11-31)

11. And the LORD spake unto Moses saying,

12. Speak unto the children of Israel, and say unto them, If any man's wife go aside, and commit a trespass against him,

13. And a man lie with her carnally, and it be hid from the eyes of her husband, and be kept close, and she be defiled, and there be no witness against her, neither she be taken with the manner;

14. And the spirit of jealousy come upon him, and he be jealous of his wife, and she be defiled: or if the spirit of jealousy come upon him, and he be jealous of his wife, and she be not defiled;

15. Then shall the man bring his wife unto the priest, and he shall bring her offering for her, the tenth part of an ephah of barley meal; he shall pour no oil upon it, nor put frankincense thereon; for it is an offering of jealousy, an offering of memorial, bringing iniquity to remembrance.

This pungent paragraph concerns a wife suspected of adultery. No positive sin or defilement is in view, only the suspicion of it—suspicion of sin.

The offering was an offering of *barley meal* and *not* fine flour as in the meal offering.

No leaven was mixed with it for that would have implied guilt before the test. *No oil or frankincense* was put on the offering for neither the presence of the Holy Spirit nor worship could be connected with an offering of jealousy.

The holy water taken by the priest was a symbol of the Word of God as the dust of the tabernacle floor was a type of death and the curse.

In this most solemn ceremony an innocent person had nothing to fear. The guilty one was found out and cursed.

Israel, as the unfaithful and adulterous wife of Jehovah, is even now under the curse.

Adultery Spells Death

1. The fine flour in these offerings typifies our Lord and Saviour Jesus Christ and hence could not be used where there was suspicion of sin.

2. Since leaven is a type of sin it could not be used in this case. Suspicion of sin is not necessarily sin. Had leaven been used it would have implied carnality and guilt.

3. Oil is a type of the Holy Spirit. An offering in connection with jealousy and a suspicion of evil therefore could not include oil. The Spirit of God is very careful in even minute matters.

4. Frankincense sets forth the intercession of Christ and the worship of saints. Since this was a case of suspicion of sin and a test of innocence or guilt, frankincense could not be allowed, for wor-

ship must be in Spirit and in truth and in the beauty of holiness.

"*The jealousy offering*—Consider the use of this law.—(1) To show the importance He attaches to domestic morality. (2) To teach them that He was looking on and knowing their most secret sins. (3) To train them to cultivate a tender conscience, and to acknowledge its authority. (4) To restore confidence between husband and wife where it was wrongly shaken (5) Though this custom is done away with, God is still the same, and will bring all secret sin into the light."—David Lloyd.

The evils of suspicion—"If thou begin to suspect evil of another, the next thing is to conclude it, and the next to report it. This suspicion is a strange shadow, that every action of another will cast upon our minds, especially if we be beforehand a little disaffected towards them. Thus, very dreams increased suspicion against Joseph in his brethren. And if once a man be out of esteem with us, let him then do what he will, be it never so virtuous and commendable, suspicion will still be the interpreter; and where suspicion is the interpreter of men's actions, slander and detraction will be the gloss and comment upon them. Indeed, suspicion is always too hasty in concluding; and many times our jealousies and distrusts, upon very small occasion, prompt us to conclude that which we have thus surmised is certainly come to pass: and so we take shadows for enemies, and report that confidently for truth which yet we never saw acted but only in our own fancies."— Bishop Hopkins.

"The trial by red water, which bears a general resemblance to that here prescribed by Moses, is still in use among the tribes of West Africa." —Spk. Com.

Illustrations

(a) "Jealousy is the bane and poison of marriage, and maketh the sociable life to be uncomfortable, and mingleth it with worse than gall and wormwood. Jealousy, therefore, is a grief of mind, arising from hence, that another is judged to enjoy that which we desire to have wholly and properly as our own, and none beside us to possess any part with us. Here, then, we cannot abide any community, but hate it as our enemy and the right cause of this jealousy. Or we may describe it otherwise on this manner: It is an affection proceeding from fear to have that communicated to another, which we challenge and covet to retain as peculiar and proper to ourselves alone. From hence it appeareth, further, what the nature of jealousy is, to wit, that it is mixed and compounded, partly of love, partly of fear, and partly of anger. Of love, which admitteth no fellow-partner in the thing he loveth: for as the king will suffer no companion to be equal unto him, or partaker with him in his kingdom, so will the husband suffer no co-rival to mate him in his love. Of fear, lest another enjoy the use of that which we cannot abide or suffer he should enjoy. Of anger, whereby it cometh to pass, that he is ready to break out to seek revenge and punishment upon him that hath offended him that way."—W. Attersoll

"Yet is there one more cursed than they all,
That canker worm, that monster, Jealousy,
Which eats the heart and feeds upon the gall,
Turning all love's delight to misery,
Through fear of losing his felicity.
Nor ever is he wont on aught to feed
But toads and frogs (his pasture poisonous),
Which, in his cold complexion, do breed
A filthy blood, or humour rancorous,
Matter of doubt and dread suspicious,
That doth with cureless care consume the heart,
Corrupt the stomach with gall vicious,
Cross-cuts the liver with eternal smart,
And doth transfix the soul with death's eternal dart."

—Edmund Spenser

(b) "The punishment of sin is not an arbitrary infliction, but it is a necessary law. Penalty is not a direct interference, but a genuine child of the transgression. We receive the things that we have done. There is a dreadful coercion in our own iniquities. There is an inevitable congruity between the deed and its consequences. There is an awful germ of identity in the seed and in the fruit.

We recognize the sown wind when we are reaping the harvest whirlwind. We feel that it is we who have winged the very arrows that eat into our hearts like fire. It needs no gathered lightnings—no divine intervention—no miraculous messenger to avenge in us God's violated laws; they avenge themselves . . . . Take disease as one form of the working of this inevitable law—not always, of course, the direct result of sin; yet how much of disease is directly due to dirt, neglect, folly, ignorance—the infected blood, the inherited instincts of this bad world. But are there not some diseases, and those the most terrible which I have known, which do spring directly, immediately, exclusively, solely, from violence of God's law? Is not madness very often such a disease? Is there not at this moment many a degraded lunatic who never would have been such but for repeated transgressions of God's known will? Is there not in the very life-blood of millions, a hereditary taint blighting the healthy, poisoning, as with a fury's breath, the flower of their happiness, and breaking out afresh in new generations, which has its sole source and origin in uncleanliness? Is there not, too, an executioner of justice which God has told off to wait upon drunkenness, which would cease if drunkenness ceased to exist? It is God's warning against that fearful intemperance against which senates will not fight, and against which they who love their fellows fight as yet in vain."—F. W. Farrer, D.D.

(c) "When Dr. Donne, afterwards Dean of St.

Paul's, took possession of the first living he ever had, he walked into the churchyard as the sexton was digging a grave; and on his throwing up a skull, the doctor took it into his hands to indulge in serious contemplation. On looking at it, he found a headless nail sticking in the temple, which he secretly drew out, and wrapped in the corner of his handkerchief. He then asked the grave digger, whether he knew whose skull it was? He said he did: adding, it had been a man's who kept a brandy shop; a drunken fellow, who, one night, having taken two quarts of ardent spirits, was found dead in his bed the next morning. 'Had he a wife?' 'Yes.' 'Is she living?' 'Yes.' 'What character does she bear?' 'A very good one; only her neighbours reflect on her because she married the day after her husband was buried.' This was enough for the doctor, who, in the course of visiting his parishioners, called on her; he asked her several questions, and, among others, of what sickness her husband died. She giving him the same account, he suddenly opened the handkerchief, and cried, in an authoritative voice. 'Woman, do you know this nail?' She was struck with horror at the unexpected question, instantly acknowledged that she had murdered her husband; and was afterwards tried and executed."—Biblical Museum

8

HOLY UNTO THE LORD

(Numbers 6:1-8)

1. And the LORD spake unto Moses, saying,

2. Speak unto the children of Israel, and say unto them, When either man or woman shall separate themselves to vow a vow of a Nazarite, to separate themselves unto the LORD:

3. He shall separate himself from wine, and strong drink, and shall drink no vinegar of wine, or vinegar of strong drink, neither shall he drink any liquor of grapes, nor eat moist grapes, or dried.

4. All the days of his separation shall he eat nothing that is made of the vine tree, from the kernels even to the husk.

5. All the days of the vow of his separation there shall no razor come upon his head: until the days be fulfilled, in the which he separateth himself unto the Lord, he shall be holy, and shall let the locks of the hair of his head grow.

6. All the days that he separateth himself unto the LORD he shall come at no dead body.

7. He shall not make himself unclean for his father, or for his mother, for his brother, or for his sister, when they die: because the consecration of his God is upon his head.

8. All the days of his separation he is holy unto the LORD.

The Nazarites of the Old Testament were to be a separated people. They were to be separated from wine, from strong drink, and from grapes. They were to be a peculiar people. No razor was to come nigh their head and they were not allowed to touch the dead whether father or mother, brother or sister, or stranger. These Old Testament Nazarites were considered a holy people. Either a man or woman could take the vow of the Nazarite. It was a voluntary act and this vow made them a peculiar, separated, and holy people.

Full salvation is voluntary. It involves separation in spirit from things that are earthly, separation from strong drink, that is, intoxicating pleasure, even separation from grapes. We are even to abstain from the very appearance of evil. The good may become the enemy of the best. It is our pleasure as well as privilege to covet the best. We too are a peculiar people, zealous of good works. Not even a father or mother, brother, sister, or stranger is to be allowed to come between us and God. See Numbers, Chapter 6.

"When either man or woman shall separate themselves."

The vow of the Nazarite was a voluntary vow. Separation and holiness are not arbitrarily bestowed upon man. Man is a free, rational, moral being and therefore may choose to go with God or the devil.

"He shall separate himself from wine and strong drink."

Wine and strong drink are symbols of earthly joys and pleasures. The godly Nazarite finds all his joy, happiness, and satisfaction in God and the things of God.

"Nor eat moist grapes or dried."

The Nazarite not only abstains from all merely earthly, worldly pleasures, but he has no delight in anything that appears to be worldly or savours of the world.

"There shall no razor come upon his head."

According to I Corinthians 11:14 it is a shame for a man to have long hair. The Nazarite must die to natural dignities and be willing to be called *peculiar*. He must give up his reputation and rights and walk among men as a separated and holy one.

"He shall come at no dead body."

No fellowship with sinners was possible or permissible without forfeiting his separation. Unsaved loved ones or relatives were not allowed to interfere with his fellowship with God. He must not tone down, round the corners, or compromise, even for his father or mother, brother or sister. "He shall not make himself unclean for his father, or for his mother, for his brother, or for his sister, when they die: because the consecration of his God is upon his head" (Numbers 6:7).

"He shall be holy."

Holiness is no new thing. I believe in holiness because I believe in a Holy God. I believe in holiness because I believe in a Holy Trinity. I believe in holiness because I believe in a Holy Heaven. I believe in holiness because I believe that only holy people could enjoy a Holy God in a Holy Heaven. Adam was created holy. Holiness is the key word of the third book of Moses, i.e., the book of Leviticus. I believe in a Holy Bible, which commands saints to be holy (I Peter 1:15-16), and which assures us that without holiness no man shall see the LORD (Heb. 12:14).

The true Nazarite was to *willingly* give up everything that tended to defile, distract, or hinder him in his communion with God. He was to abstain from all earthly joys, surrender the dignities of nature, and be holy unto the Lord. "And if any man die very suddenly by him, and he hath defiled the head of his consecration; then he shall shave his head in the day of his cleansing, on the seventh day shall he shave it. And on the eighth day he shall bring two turtles, or two young pigeons, to the priest, to the door of the tabernacle of the congregation: And the priest shall offer the one for a sin offering, and the other for a burnt offering, and make an atonement for him, for that he sinned by the dead, and shall hallow his head that same day. And he shall consecrate unto the LORD the days of his separation, and shall bring a lamb of the first year for a trespass offering; for the days that were before shall be lost, because his separation was defiled" (Num. 6:9-12). These verses show clearly that sin and defilement are dreadful things in the sight of God. One sin brought about the ruin of the race of man. Sin brought the flood which in judgment swept the wicked race from the earth, and which in mercy gave a fresh start through Noah and his family. Sin brought fire and brimstone upon the unholy heads of the Sodomites. Sin opened the earth to swallow Korah, Dathan, Abiram and On. These men went alive into hell as Enoch and Elijah went alive into heaven. One sin caused the first tragedy in the Apostolic Church, the tragedy of Ananias and his wife. They were knocked down in the meeting house and died by the judgments of God. Sin is a fearful thing in the sight of God. It is a leprosy that pollutes. It is a consumption that wastes. It is a cancer that destroys. It has drenched the earth with blood and filled it with the bones of the dead and dying. The very earth groans under the weight of man's sin. Either sin must be destroyed, or sin will destroy the person in whose breast it is allowed to remain. Sin is a dreadful thing in God's sight.

"He shall be holy, and shall let the locks of the hair of his head grow. All the days that he separateth himself unto the Lord, he shall come at no dead body."

"Those that separate themselves to God, must learn to keep their consciences pure from dead works, and not to touch the unclean thing. The greater profession of religion we make, and the more eminent we appear, the greater care we must take to avoid all sin, for we have so much the more honour to lose by it."—M. Henry

"Under the Levitical law, the touch of any dead body rendered the person ceremonially unclean; but this uncleanness was especially aggravated by the touch of a human dead body; for death came in by sin, and was thus accounted unclean, till the death, burial, and resurrection of Christ, as it were, sanctified death and the grave to his people. But the soul, dead in sin, and the dead works attending that state, are still as polluted and polluting as ever."—Scott

9

A BIBLE BENEDICTION

"The LORD bless thee."

(Numbers 6:22-27)

22. And the LORD spake unto Moses, saying,

23. Speak unto Aaron and unto his sons, saying, On this wise ye shall bless the children of Israel, saying unto them,

24. The LORD bless thee, and keep thee;

25. The LORD make his face shine upon thee, and be gracious unto thee:

26. The LORD lift up his countenance upon thee, and give thee peace.

27. And they shall put my name upon the children of Israel; and I will bless them.

Man needs a sacred Sabbath in each week of his work for himself and others. He also needs to acknowledge his indebtedness to God by paying tithes of all his income and increase. To attend the Lord's house on the Lord's day and to take the Lord's tithe with him intact, and inviolate is a sacred part of divine worship. Man also needs the sacred seasons of prayer and communion and fellowship with God and with those of like precious faith. Man is a needy creature. He also needs blessings and benedictions such as the one in Numbers 6.

No argument is needed to prove the divine inspiration of these wonderful words of life, peace, and power.

"The Lord bless thee." For wonderful words which bring sweet solaces into the heart's heaviness, the language of the Old Testament Scriptures are unexcelled. There is sweet and strengthening wine in every word of these sacred Scriptures. In and through all the agonies of the human heart these beautiful words bring a healing balm.

A good and gracious God marked out the land, planned the hedges, and arranged for the fixing of the fences. He purposefully led his people out of the bondage of Egypt and away from the follies and sin of Pharaoh and, having fed them with angels' food, now talks of blessing, keeping, and shining. God ushers the converted, cleansed, and consecrated soul into a new clime. He is bent on blessing the believer with all spiritual blessings in heavenly places. We may put in a bid for our portion.

Here is the Lord's prayer of the Old Testament and being the Lord's prayer, it is perfect and complete. The sacred name occurs three times in these thirty-two words. It is therefore not only a perfect and complete prayer, but a perfect and complete benediction. It is a benediction from the Triune Benefactor and Blesser.

No believer should be satisfied to live an unblest life. God sends the dew upon the grass and clothes the lily. Much more will he send his dew upon you and clothe you. "The Lord bless thee!"

Here is set forth the trinity of blessing.

1. Through a Mediator
   Moses as mediator was a type of Christ.
2. After atonement had been made
   Aaron the high priest making an atonement also was a type of Christ.
3. The threefold blessing was to be a *personal* blessing.
   "The LORD bless *thee.*"
4. A divine blessing
   "The LORD bless thee."
5. A *preserving* blessing.
   "The LORD bless thee and *keep thee.*"
6. An *illuminating* blessing.
   "And cause his face to *shine upon* thee."
7. A *peace bestowing* blessing.
   "And give thee *peace.*"

"In the benediction with which this chapter closes, the word Jehovah is three times solemnly repeated; and the Jews themselves have supposed, that there is some great mystery contained in that repetition. When we compare it with the form of Christian baptism—'Into the name of the Father, and of the Son, and of the Holy Ghost'—with the blessing that St. Paul pronounced on the Corinthians, which is in common use in our places of worship; and with John's salutation of the churches (Rev. 1:4-5), we can be at no loss to determine what that mystery is. Sinners are blessed with spiritual blessings by the triune God of salvation; the Father who chose, the Son who redeemed, and the Holy Spirit who sanctifies and comforts all the elect people of God."—Scott.

"This blessing, according to Rabbi Menachen, was pronounced in a different accent, during the utterance of each part; and, according to an account given by two other Rabbies, with the hand lifted up, and the first three fingers of the hand extended; the little finger being at the same time closed. This, they say, was done to express a trial or trinity, in the Godhead."—Dwight

10

SEVEN WAYS OF GIVING TO GOD

(Numbers 6:30-35; 7:1-89)

Chapter seven is the longest chapter in the book of Numbers. It describes in minute detail the offerings of the princes. The name and service of each Levite is thus eternally preserved. Each Levite has his day, and each offering is recorded. Nothing is omitted. Nothing is passed over hastily. Man may pass lightly over the gifts and offerings of God's people and say little or nothing about tithes, but God is different. Every little act and every loving gift is recorded and remembered and eternally rewarded. As the widow giving her two mites was noticed by the Son of God and the offering remembered and eternally preserved, so a cup of cold water shall not fail in its reward if given in the name of a disciple and for the glory of that disciple's God. Read Numbers 7 and be encouraged to bring your tithes and offerings and leave them at the place of consecration and prayer. Here in this longest chapter we find that every item is minutely and faithfully recorded. The smallest gift and the slightest service is remembered by God and everlastingly preserved. Written in God's Book is the record of all the sacrifice, self-denial, and sorrows of all God's saints. It is at once interesting and instructive to notice that in the last verse God manifested himself to Moses. After this tremendous offering, God fellowships Moses. The offering apparently gave wings to the wishes of God's people and brought God down to commune with his chosen.

Seven Ways of Giving—(1) *The careless way*—To give something to every cause that is presented without inquiring into its merits. (2) *The impulsive way*—To give from impulse—as much and as often as love and pity and sensibility prompt. (3) *The lazy way*—To make a special effort to earn money for benevolent objects by fairs, festivals, etc. (4) *The self-denying way*—To save the cost of luxuries and apply them to purposes of religion and charity. This may lead to asceticism and self-complacence. (5) *The systematic way*—To lay aside as an offering to God a definite portion of our gains—one-tenth, one-fifth, one-third, or one-half. This is adapted to all, whether poor or rich; and gifts would be largely increased if it were generally practiced. (6) *The equal way*—To give to God and the needy just as much as we spend on ourselves, balancing our personal expenditure by our gifts. (7) *The heroic way*— To limit our expenses to a certain sum, and give away all the rest of our income. This was John Wesley's way.

Motives for Giving to God—"When we do give, in what spirit and with what feeling is it? Oh, my brethren! put down what you give from vanity, that your name may appear creditably along with others; put down what you give from indolence, because you are entreated to do so, and in order to rid yourself of those troublesome applicants; put down what you are surprised into giving, and in reality give with regret, like one who submits to a disagreeable necessity when he is not skilful enough to avoid it; put down what you give through weakness, from no other motive than the purely negative one that you had not the courage to refuse; put down what you give in ill-humor, secretly indulging angry feelings either against those who have appealed to you, or those on whose behalf the appeal has been made; then put down what you give cheerfully, and in the spirit of those words of Jesus, 'It is more blessed to give than to receive.' "—Dr. Coulin

Giving

We might all of us give far more than we do,
Without being a bit the worse;
It was never yet loving that emptied the heart,
Nor giving that emptied the purse.

The sun gives ever; so the earth—
What it can give so much 'tis worth;
The ocean gives in many ways—
Gives paths, gives fishes, rivers, bays;
So, too, the air, it gives us breath—
When it stops giving, comes in death.

Give, give, be always giving:
Who gives not is not living.
The more you give,
The more you live.

God's love hath to us wealth upheaped;
Only by giving it is reaped.
The body withers, and the mind,
If pent in by selfish rind,
Give strength, give thought, give deeds, give pelf,
Give love, give tears, and give thyself;
Give, give, be always giving
Who gives not is not living
The more we give,
The more we live.

"An Irish bishop having lost his way, once called at the cottage of a poor woman for direction, when he found her just finishing her dinner of cold water and a crust of dry bread, but, in the height of thankfulness, praising God as if in the midst of unbounded mercies, as she said, 'What, have all this and Christ besides!' "—Bowes

"There are some men that give as springs do. Whether you go to them or not, they are always full; and your part is merely to put your dish under the ever-flowing stream. Others give just as a pump does, where the well is dry and the pump leaks."—Beecher

"A bountiful giver.—In Scotland I was attend-

ing a missionary meeting, and you know in Scotland it is the fashion to give money at the door coming in or going out. Going away from the meeting, a poor servant came and dropped in a sovereign. The deacon standing there said, 'I am sure you can't afford to give that.' 'Oh! yes, I can.' 'You will have to go without clothes.' 'Oh! no, I shan't.' 'Do take it back,' he said. She replied, 'I must give it.' The deacon then said, 'Take it home tonight, and if, after thinking of it during the night, you choose to give it, you can send it.' The next morning I sat at breakfast, and there was a little note came, and it contained two sovereigns. The good deacon said, 'You won't take it!' I said, 'Of course I shall, for if I send it back, she will send four next time'."—Scott

"Thou must be emptied of self before thou canst be filled with the Spirit."—Thornton

Giving to God repaid—John Wesley and a servant, when traveling, stopped at a house of a poor woman who had just lost her cow, and who was brokenhearted because it was her only means of support. Wesley asked his servant how much money they had, and he replied, "Fifty dollars." "Give it all to the woman," said he. They journeyed on, and the next place they stopped at the people handed him ninety dollars. Wesley in surprise turned to his servant and said, "How is this? There ought to be one hundred, for we gave away fifty," "Ah," said the servant, "I did not dare give the woman more than forty-five; I thought we ought to keep five dollars for ourselves!"

Give cheerfully.—

Give! as the morning that flows out of heaven;
Give! as the waves when their channel is riven;
Give! as the free air and sunshine are given;
Lavishly, utterly, joyfully give.
Not the waste drops of thy cup overflowing,
Not the faint sparks of thy hearth ever glowing,
Not a pale bud from the June roses blowing;
Give as He gave thee who gave thee to live.

Benefits of liberality—"I never prospered more in my small estate than when I gave most, and needed least. My own rule hath been, first, to contrive to need myself as little as may be, and lay out none on need-nots, but to live frugally on a little; second, to serve God in my place, upon that competency which He allowed me to myself, that what I had myself might be as good a work for common good as that which I gave to others; and, third, to do all the good I could with all the rest, preferring the most public and the most durable object, and the nearest. And, the more I have practiced this, the more I have had to do it with; and when I gave almost all, more came in (without any gift), I scarce knew how, at least unexpected; but when my improvidence I have cast myself into necessities of using more upon myself, or upon things in themselves of less importance, I have prospered much less than when I did otherwise. And when I had contented myself to devote that stock which I had gotten to charitable uses after my death, instead of laying out at present, that so I might secure somewhat for myself while I lived, in probability all that is like to be lost; whereas, when I took that present opportunity, and trusted God for the time to come, I wanted nothing, and lost nothing."—R. Baxter

Sydney Smith recommends it as a rule, to try to make at least one person happy every day, and adds the calculation—take ten years, and you will have made three thousand six hundred and fifty persons happy, or brightened a small town by your contribution to the fund of general joy.

11

THE TABERNACLE

(Numbers 8:1-26)

I. Names

1. Tabernacle of the *congregation*
2. Tabernacle of the *Lord*
3. Tabernacle of the *testimony*
4. Tabernacle of the *witness*

The tabernacle was thus for *use by the children of Israel.* It was *God's dwelling place.* In it were *two tables of stone,* and *Aaron's rod was a witness* against the rebels.

II. The Outer Court

1. Hangings

   These were of fine linen, a type of Christ's righteousness.

2. The Pillars

   These pillars with feet of brass and silver capitals set forth the firmness, stability, and steadfastness of Christ, which support his righteousness.

III. The Gate

This was the entrance to the court and was called the gate. The entrance to the Holy place was called the door while the entrance to the holy of holies was called the vail.

"Strait is the gate."

"I am the door."

"The veil . . . . his flesh."

There was only *one* gate, *one* door and *one* vail. Cain attempted to gain access in his own way and was rejected.

IV. The Material of the Gate

1. Blue

   Blue is the color of the sky and sets forth a heavenly Christ—"God manifest in flesh."

2. Purple

   This is the royal color and speaks of Christ as God's chosen king, the kingly Christ.

3. Scarlet

   Here is typified the Man of Sorrows, the Man dying for the sins of all.

4. Fine Linen

   Fine linen represents the righteous life of Jesus Christ. These colors are mentioned over twenty times in the book of Exodus alone, and the order never varies.

V. The Brazen Altar

This altar was made of wood and covered with brass. Wood sets forth the *humanity* of Christ while the brass sets forth his *justice*. Brass is one of the most unbending and unyielding of substances. The brazen altar was twice the size of the ark of the covenant and in fact was large enough to contain all the other vessels of the Sanctuary. We may learn here that every blessing which is ours for time and eternity is comprehended in the one supreme sacrifice of Christ on the cross. It was impossible to obtain *access to God* without first approaching the brazen altar, where the innocent victims were offered. Without shedding of blood there is no access to God and no remission of sins.

VI. The Horns of the Altar

These horns pointed in every direction, inviting the *whosoever will* to lay hold on the hope set before him. The horns were used to bind the sacrifice to the Altar, and was it not love, rather than nails that bound the strong Son of God to the cross of shame?

VII. The Fire

Fire is the sign and symbol of God. Our God is a consuming fire. This fire was a divine fire. "And there came a fire out from before the Lord, and consumed upon the altar the burnt offering and the fat" (Lev. 9:24a)

This fire was a perpetual fire. "The fire shall ever be burning upon the altars; it shall never go out" (Lev. 6:13). Bible religion is a religion of blood and fire.

The standard of the Salvation Army was the standard of Israel 4,000 years before William Booth was born.

It is instructive to notice that the network of brass called the grate, through which the ashes of the victim fell, was on a level with the mercy seat in the holy of holies.

VIII. The Laver

The laver was made out of the brazen mirrors of the women. From these instruments of self-admiration, which were conducive to vanity and pride, there was formed a laver, which reminded them of their pollution and their need of cleansing before they could obtain nearness to God. "For if any be a hearer of the word, and not a doer, he is like unto a man beholding his natural face in a glass: For he beholdeth himself, and goeth his way, and straightway forgetteth what manner of man he was. But whoso looketh into the perfect law of liberty, and continueth therein, he being not a forgetful hearer, but a doer of the work, 1:23-25).

The altar says, "Christ died for our sins," while the laver demands "clean hands." The hands and feet symbolize the whole life of the believer. At the cross (brazen altar) we are justified, and at the laver we are kept from the daily pollution of a sinful world as we walk according to the Word.

IX. The Door

This door was made of blue, purple, scarlet, and fine linen. It was suspended on five pillars, setting forth the (1) Wonderful, (2) Counsellor, (3) Mighty God, (4) Everlasting Father, and (5) Prince of Peace.

It would remind us of (1) the King, (2) eternal, (3) immortal, (4) invisible, and (5) the only wise God.

Christ is the one and the only way to God, the only door, for we are merely (1) apostles, (2) prophets, (3) evangelists, (4) pastors, (5) teachers. "And he gave some, apostles; and some, prophets; and some, evangelists; and some, pastors and teachers; For the perfecting of the saints, for the work of the ministry, for the edifying of the body of Christ." (Eph. 4:11-12). These pillars were crowned with gold. As wood speaks of the humanity of Christ so gold sets forth his deity. Although uncrowned in life, save in mockery and with thorns, nevertheless he is God's chosen king. The door was for the priest. Only those who pray know the sweetness of fellowship at the table of bread called the shewbread.

X. The Candlestick

This lampstick or candlestick was made of pure gold. The *light of the world* is a divine light. The branches and shaft were beaten out of a solid slab of gold, thus setting forth the sufferings of God. The branches had no standing or light apart from the main shaft. "I am the vine, ye are the branches; He that abideth in me, and I in him, the same bringeth forth much fruit: for without me ye can do nothing" (John 15:5).

There were many lamps, but there was only one light. The priests accomplished their work, not by reason or by the light of nature, but by the light of the candlestick. Christ is the light of life. No extinguisher was provided, for the light was to burn and shine by day and by night. Christ is the light of the world, and believers are to let their lights shine.

XI. The Table of Shewbread

Christ is the bread of God, the bread of angels, and the bread of life. The cakes of fine flour exhibit the evenness and smoothness of Christ's life. This bread was changed every Sabbath. God's ministers are to feed on fresh bread. Life cannot be sustained on past experiences or past blessings.

XII. The Altar of Incense

This altar was the highest of all the vessels in the tabernacle. It was made of wood and overlaid with pure gold. A crown of pure gold encircled it.

"Wherefore he is able also to save them to the

uttermost that come unto God by him, seeing he ever liveth to make intercession for them" (Heb. 7:25).

XIII. The Veil

The veil concealed the presence of God.

The veil hindered the people from seeing God.

The veil was a type of the human Christ. "Having therefore, brethren, boldness to enter into the holiest by the blood of Jesus, By a new and living way, which he hath consecrated for us, through the veil; that is to say, his flesh" (Heb. 10:19-20).

The veil was the only way into the presence of God. "Jesus saith unto him, I am the way, the truth, and the life; no man cometh to the Father, but by me" (John 14:6).

When Christ died, the veil was rent in twain from "top to the bottom," thus showing that redemption was all of God and from God. Believers now have access into the very presence of God.

XIV. The Ark

1. Ark of Testimony

"There will I meet with thee, and I will commune with thee from above the mercy seat, from between the two cherubims which are upon the ark of the testimony, of all things which I will give thee in commandment unto the children of Israel" (Exodus 25:22).

2. Ark of Covenant

. . . . "the ark of the covenant of the LORD went before them in the three days' journey, to search out a resting place for them" (Numbers 10:33).

3. Ark of the Lord

"And unto Abiathar the priest said the king, Get thee to Anathoth, unto thine own fields; for thou art worthy of death: but I will not at this time put thee to death, because thou barest the ark of the Lord God before David my father, and because thou hast been afflicted in all wherein my father was afflicted" (I Kings 2:26).

4. Ark of God

"And ere the lamp of God went out in the temple of the LORD, where the ark of God was, and Samuel was laid down to sleep" (I Sam. 3:3).

5. Ark of God's Strength

"Arise, O LORD, into thy rest; thou, and the ark of thy strength" (Psa. 132.8).

XV. Contents of the Ark

1. Within the ark there were the unbroken tablets of the law.

Christ kept the perfect law of God and kept it for us.

2. Pot of Manna

   Manna was wilderness food and typified Christ as the bread of God and the bread of life come down from heaven.

3. Aaron's Rod

   The dry stick speaks of Christ in death, while the blossoming and budding sets forth Christ in resurrection power and glory.

4. Several miracles were performed because of the presence of the ark.
   (1) Jordan divided
   (2) Walls of Jericho fell flat
   (3) Fall of Dagon
   (4) Philistines plagued
   (5) The ark now is in heaven. "And the temple of God was opened in heaven, and there was seen in his temple the ark of his testament" (Rev. 11:19a). The ark thus typified a miracle working divine-human Christ, who is even now in heaven.

XVI. The Mercy Seat

The word mercyseat means "a covering" and signified a covering of sin by forgiveness. This forgiveness and covering was on the sole ground of accepted sacrifice. "Whom God hath set forth to be a propitiation through faith in his blood, to declare his righteousness for the remission of sins that are past, through the forbearance of God" (Rom. 3:25). This was the only meeting place between a holy God and unholy man. This was the only place of communion between a saving God and a sinful man.

"Let us therefore come boldly unto the throne of grace, that we may obtain mercy, and find grace to help in time of need" (Heb. 4:16).

XVII. The Cherubims

The cherubims are first mentioned in Genesis 3:24. "So he drove out the man; and he placed at the east of the garden of Eden, Cherubims, and a flaming sword which turned every way, to keep the way of the tree of life." Ezekiel twice mentions the Cherubim, which word is simply the plural for Cherub, which means "to shine." They are a part of the veil and thus are connected with Christ in his atoning work.

I am satisfied in my own heart that the Cherubim typify the Church of Jesus Christ. They are emblematical of redeemed man, redeemed in Christ before the foundation of the world. Their outspreading wings set forth the fact that saints are a heavenly, rather than an earthly, people. We are even now pilgrims and strangers.

The fact that they were beaten out of pure gold speaks of the divine nature imputed and imparted to the people of God. It also shows that as we suffer with him we shall also reign with him. Looking down upon the sprinkled blood, and the mercy seat testifies that we are always in need of atoning blood, and that from first to last "salvation is in the blood" of Christ and through the mercy of God.

Since they stand on the mercy seat we may learn that redemption is all of God's grace and that Christ's death is our only place of rest, safety, and security.

XVIII. The Boards

The boards rested on sockets of silver. The boards were typical of believers who stand on redemption ground. The silver was the atonement money of the people. Take away the silver sockets and all would rest and depend on the shifting sands of the desert. The only safe foundation is Christ.

12

THE PILLAR OF CLOUD

(Numbers 9:15-23)

The cloud by day and the fire by night which covered and protected the tabernacle was a symbol of the presence of the Holy Spirit with his people. The Spirit was present and with the Father and the Son created the heaven and the earth in the beginning. (See Gen. 1:1.) The Spirit moved upon the face of the waters in the great restoration plans and purposes of God after sin had marred his handiwork. (See Gen. 1:2.) The dove sent out by Noah was a type of the Holy Spirit who cannot rest where there is only destruction and death. The servant of Abraham (Eliezer) is a clear and plain foreshadowing of the Holy Spirit as he seeks a bride for the well beloved son. That he is more than a type of the gospel minister will be admitted by all except the prejudiced and jaundiced. The story of Joseph's steward is a story of surpassing beauty and grandeur to all who have ears to hear and hearts to understand. Joseph's steward is a clear prefiguring of the Holy Spirit in his work of winning the brethren of Joseph, the Jews. Joshua and Elisha were both types of the Spirit. The history of the cloud which covered the tabernacle will repay careful and prolonged study.

Israel was to watch the cloud and move, march, stop and go with it. To watch for the movings and marchings, stoppings and goings of the Holy Spirit is a fine art. To mind his checks, yield to his gentle entreaties, and listen to his voice means profit and blessing, growth and glory while travelling the holy way.

The cloud was (1) a supernatural cloud, (2) adapted to both night and day, (3) reliable, (4) plainly pointed the right way, (5) mysterious in its movements, (6) a comforting cloud, (7) constant, stable and light giving, (8) to follow meant life and peace.

"At the commandment of the Lord they rested in the tents, and at the commandment of the Lord they journeyed: they kept the charge of the Lord, at the commandment of the Lord by the hand of Moses."

"The case of two or three millions of people, shut up in a dreary wilderness for almost 40 years, without ever seeing house, or garden, or cornfield; as completely, as if the highest walls, garrisoned by the most valiant troops, had surrounded them; compared with their rebellions in other things, and their submission in this respect; most strikingly shows, that they were convinced beyond the possibility of doubt, that resistance must be unavailing: Yet nothing short of having witnessed the miracles recorded in these books could have induced this strong conviction."—Scott

"This spirit of submission should be imitated too by the spiritual Israelites: they ought not to undertake anything from their own will, lest confusion and disappointment should encompass every path. The unconverted are full of their own will; how should they succeed? They are bewildered here, and run into perdition eternally. Sometimes the faithful may, with a good design, when they are engaged in a good work, outrun the will of God, and not wait for his counsel. O God! grant that in all things, even in my best works, I may be guided by thine eye, and wait for thy counsel with a resigned temper! May I speak, or be silent, work or rest, when, and as thou wilt! then shall my ways be blest, and thou wilt never leave me nor forsake me."—Bogatzky

13

THE SILVER TRUMPETS

(Numbers 10:1-10)

1. And the Lord spake unto Moses, saying,

2. Make thee two trumpets of silver; of a whole piece shalt thou make them : that thou mayest use them for the calling of the assembly, and for the journeying of the camps.

3. And when they shall blow with them, all the assembly shall assemble themselves to thee at the door of the tabernacle of the congregation.

4. And if they blow but with one trumpet, then the princes, which are heads of the thousands of Israel, shall gather themselves unto thee.

5. When ye blow an alarm, then the camps that lie on the east parts shall go forward.

6. When ye blow an alarm the second time, then the camps that lie on the south side shall take their journey: they shall blow an alarm for their journeys.

7. But when the congregation is to be gathered together, ye shall blow, but ye shall not sound an alarm.

8. And the sons of Aaron, the priests, shall blow with the trumpets; and they shall be to you for an ordinance for ever throughout your generations.

9. And if ye go to war in your land against the enemy that oppresseth you, then ye shall blow an alarm with the trumpets; and ye shall be remembered before the LORD your God, and ye shall be saved from your enemies.

10. Also in the day of your gladness, and in your solemn days, and in the beginnings of your months, ye shall blow with the trumpets over your burnt offerings, and over the sacrifices of your peace offerings; that they may be to you for a memorial before your God: I am the LORD your God.

The trumpets typify the Word of God, the gospel of our salvation. They were to be blown by the priest, those separated and sanctified to such service. All believers are now priests. They are to be separated, consecrated, and sanctified to the making known the glad, full and good news of salvation. "Ye are my witnesses." With the heart man believeth unto righteousness and with the mouth confession is made unto salvation." (See Rom. 10:9-10.) What God hath joined together let no man put asunder. These trumpets made no uncertain sounds and believers are to be definite and implicit in their testimonies. The silver trumpets were used in calling the people to advance. We are to arise and go forward in the warfare against the world, the flesh, and the devil. There should be daily advancement in personal holiness, usefulness, and blessing.

The trumpets were also used to encourage

the people in battle. Our warfare is not against flesh and blood, but against Satan, evil spirits, the flesh within, and the corrupt world without. The people of God need constant encouragement in this terrific and titantic struggle against sin and all unholiness.

We must continue to encourage the saints to fight against evil, to mortify the flesh, to crucify self, to keep under the body, and to resist the devil.

The silver (redemption) trumpets (testimony) were also to sound "in the day of gladness" at Sunday school parties and picnics, thanksgiving festivities, Christmas, New Year, and Halloween, etc. We must not forget God in our days of gladness.

14

THE MURMURING OF MIRIAM

(Numbers 12:1-6a)

1. And Miriam and Aaron spake against Moses because of the Ethiopian woman whom he had married; for he had married an Ethiopian woman.

2. And they said, Hath the LORD indeed spoken only by Moses? hath he not spoken also by us? And the LORD heard it.

3. (Now the man Moses was very meek, above all the men which were upon the face of the earth.)

4. And the LORD spake suddenly unto Moses, and unto Aaron, and unto Miriam, Come out ye three unto the tabernacle of the congregation. And they three came out.

5. And the LORD came down in the pillar of the cloud, and stood in the door of the tabernacle, and called Aaron and Miriam: and they both came forth.

6a. And he said, Hear now my words.

God graciously met with and wondrously blessed his people. After the miraculous crossing of the Red Sea, Miriam danced for joy and led the women in a praise the Lord campaign. Somewhere along the line, however, Miriam became lukewarm and her singing and dancing ceased.

"Miriam spake unto Moses." The Holy Spirit was grieved and Miriam became leprous. Green-eyed jealousy, envy, and malice had been encouraged in her heart and almost imperceptibly she had become a character killer, and that of her own brother. Birds of a feather flock together and soon Miriam and Aaron spoke against Moses. Faultfinders seek other faultfinders. As a moth gnaws a garment, so envy and jealousy consume the soul. Like a soaring and roaring flame, evil speaking blackens that which is above it, and which it cannot reach. Miriam and Aaron little realized that a third party was present and listening. "And the Lord heard." There is always a third party present when things are said and done which ought not to be said or done. God hears and some day it shall be repeated from the housetops, for be sure sin will find us out.

Moses refused to fuss or fight either for himself or his rights and consequently the Lord stepped in and took up the fight for him. "And the anger of the Lord was kindled against them." God is angry with every character killer and reputation ruiner. "And he departed from them." God refused to stay longer with this evil speaking duet. Miriam talked God out of her heart and life. Aaron gossiped God out of the temple of his soul. Not only did God depart from them, however, but (1) The cloud departed from off the tabernacle, (2) Miriam was leprous, (3) Miriam was shut out, and (4) the people journeyed not. It is a serious thing to slander God's servants. God refused to hear even the prayer of a Moses on behalf of Miriam. Miriam was shut out. The work of God was stopped.

"Now the man Moses was very meek, above all the men which were upon the face of the earth."

"Several of the sacred writers have spoken of themselves, as enabled by divine grace to act with great integrity and holiness in most trying circumstances, yet without any vain glory or ostentation. And our Lord says of himself, 'I am meek and lowly in heart.' It is, therefore, a senseless cavil to adduce this declaration, as a proof that Moses was not the author of this book in opposition to the unanimous tradition of antiquity, and the testimony of Christ and his apostles in the New Testament. As Moses was meek, it was the more necessary that the Lord should plead his cause. Being singularly meek above all men, he took no notice of the affairs, to resent it, or to punish any persons for their misconduct."—Scott

"There is no reason why the meek should not be also valiant. The man who girds himself up to some noble and difficult service, is, of all others, the one least likely largely to promise what he will do, or loudly to boast of what he has done." —Anon

"In the great battle of life, there are some men who remain withdrawn from the fierceness of the struggle, in a retired and sheltered part of the field. They think this proves them to be meek; yet it is quite possible, it may only prove them to be cowards; for there is a false meekness which consists in submitting to be driven, because we have not the courage to drive."—Ibid

"No might nor greatness in mortality
Can censure 'scape; back-wounding calumny
The whitest virtue strikes: What king so strong,
Can tie the gall up in the slanderous tongue,"
——Shakespeare.

Patience under injustice. Rowland Hill, when once scurrilously attacked in one of the public journals, was urged by a zealous friend to bring a legal action in defense: to this he replied with calm, unruffled dignity—"I shall neither answer the libel, nor prosecute the writer, and that for two reasons: first, because, in attempting the former, I should probably be betrayed into unbecoming violence of temper and expression, to my own grief, and the wounding of my friends; and in the next place, I have learned by experience that no man's character can be eventually injured by his own acts."—Gleanings

"And he said, Hear now my words: If there be a prophet among you, I the LORD will make myself known unto him in a vision, and will speak unto him in a dream. My servant Moses is not so, who is faithful in all mine house. With him will I speak mouth to mouth, even apparently, and not in dark speeches; and the similitude of the LORD shall he behold: wherefore then were ye not afraid to speak against my servant Moses? And the anger of the LORD was kindled against them; and he departed" (Numbers 12:6-9).

Condition of Communion. "Birds cannot converse with men unless they have a rational nature put into them; nor can men converse with God, unless, being made new creatures, they partake of the divine nature. Communion with God is a mystery to most. Every one that hangs about the court doth not speak with the king; all that meddle with holy duties, and, as it were, hang about the court of heaven, have not communion with God; it is only the new creature enjoys God's presence in ordinances, and sweetly converses with him as a child with a father."—T. Watson

"And the cloud departed from off the tabernacle; and, behold, Miriam became leprous, white as snow: and Aaron looked upon Miriam, and, behold, she was leprous" (Numbers 12:10).

"Deformity is a fit cure of pride. Because the venom of Miriam's tongue would have eaten into the reputation of her brother, therefore a poisonous infection ate into her flesh. Now both Moses and Miriam needed to wear a veil, the one to hide his glory, and the other her deformity. That Midianite Zipporah, whom she scorned, was now beautiful in comparison to her." Bp. Hall

"Under such humbling providences, we ought

to be very humble. It is a sign the heart is hard indeed, if the flesh be mortified, and yet the lusts of the flesh remain unmortified."—M. Henry

"And Aaron said unto Moses, Alas, my lord, I beseech thee, lay not the sin upon us, wherein we have done foolishly, and wherein we have sinned. Let her not be as one dead, of whom the flesh is half consumed when he cometh out of his mother's womb. And Moses cried unto the LORD, saying, Heal her now, O God, I beseech thee. And the LORD said unto Moses, If her father had but spit in her face, should she not be ashamed seven days? let her be shut out from the camp seven days, and after that let her be received in again. And Miriam was shut out from the camp seven days: and the people journeyed not till Miriam was brought in again" (Numbers 12:11-15).

"The prayer of Moses for Miriam—Consider the prayer. How conclusively does it attest the excellency of the character of Moses! How worthy of power is one so large-hearted and forgiving. The prayer was—(1) Explicit. Nothing vague. He prays not for wrong-doers in the mass, but for one in particular, and that one who had wronged him. Many will pray general prayers heartily enough. Lips, willing to say, 'Have mercy on us, miserable sinners,' refuse to say, 'Lord, be merciful to me, a sinner'; (2) Earnest. Did he see the Shekinah receding (vs. 10), and would have God return at once? God's withdrawals excit prayer; (3) Gen-

erous: 'Heal her now.' Not make her penitent, or cause her to beg forgiveness, and then heal her, or remove the disease after a certain time; but 'Heal her now'; (4) Well-timed. He waited not till the memory of her sin and his wrong were fainter; at once his cry goes us. We are not 'to give place unto wrath.' He gives place who gives time."—R. A. Griffin

"*Consciousness of guilt.* However vauntingly men may bear themselves in the hour of prosperous villainy, proofs enough have existed of the fears of guilt, when the hour of calamity approaches. Why did our first parents hide themselves after their sin, when they heard the voice of the Lord in the garden? Why did Cain alarm himself at being pursued by the people of the earth? Why shrunk Belshazzar from the handwriting on the wall? Adam had before heard the voice of the Lord, and trembled not; Cain knew that no witness of the murder of his brother existed; Belshazzar understood not the meaning of the writing upon the wall;—and yet they all, after the commission of their several deeds of sin, trembled at the voices that were heard, and the signs that were seen. Whence, then, was this? It was because conscience told them that there is an Eye to which all hearts are open, and whispered the important truth, which has since been proclaimed aloud to all the world, that, doubtless there is a God that judgeth the earth.' "—Matthews

"Conscience is harder than our enemies,
Knows more, accuses with more nicety,
Nor needs to question Rumor if we fall
Below the perfect model of our thought."
—Geo. Eliot

"Guilt, though it may attain temporal splendor, can never confer real happiness. The evident consequences of our crimes, long survive their commission and, like the ghosts of the murdered, forever haunt the steps of the malefactor. The paths of virtue, though seldom those of worldly greatness, are always those of pleasantness and peace." Sir Walter Scott

"Behold her guilty looks; for guilt will speak, though tongues were out of use."—Shakespeare

15

A PEOPLE DISCIPLINED

(Numbers 14:11-24)

11. And the LORD said unto Moses, How long will this people provoke me? and how long will it be ere they believe me, for all the signs which I have showed among them?

12. I will smite them with the pestilence, and disinherit them, and will make of thee a greater nation and mightier than they.

13. And Moses said unto the LORD, Then the Egyptians shall hear it, (for thou broughtest up this people in thy might from among them;)

14. And they will tell it to the inhabitants of this land: for they have heard that thou LORD art among this people and thou Lord art seen face to face, and that thy cloud standeth over them, and that thou goest before them, by daytime in pillar of a cloud, and in a pillar of fire by night.

15. Now if thou shalt kill all this people as one man, then the nations which have heard the fame of thee will speak, saying,

16. Because the LORD was not able to bring this people into the land which he sware unto them, therefore he hath slain them in the wilderness.

17. And now, I beseech thee, let the power of my LORD be great, according as thou hast spoken, saying,

18. The LORD is long-suffering, and of great mercy, forgiving iniquity and transgression, and by no means clearing the guilty, visiting the iniquity of the fathers upon the children unto the third and fourth generations.

19. Pardon, I beseech thee, the iniquity of this people according unto the greatness of thy mercy, and as thou hast forgiven this people, from Egypt even until now.

20. And the LORD said, I have pardoned according to thy word:

21. But as truly as I live, all the earth shall be filled with the glory of the LORD.

22. Because all those men which have seen my glory, and my miracles, which I did in Egypt and in the wilderness, and have tempted me now these ten times, and have not hearkened to my voice;

23. Surely they shall not see the land which I sware unto their fathers, neither shall any of them that provoked me see it:

24. But my servant Caleb, because he had another spirit with him, and hath followed me fully, him will I bring into the land whereinto he went; and his seed shall possess it.

"The unbelieving world can appreciate only

omnipotent power. When this is withdrawn, God fails. They have no conception of the divine holiness, justice, wisdom, and truth, as influencing the government of God. That is a very shallow theology which teaches that men will be saved from hell by sheer omnipotence, without respect to character. But Moses appealed to all the moral attributes of God, and he prevailed."—Whedon's Commentary

"And now, I beseech thee, let the power of my Lord be great, according as thou hast spoken, saying," (vs. 17). "Here the argument of Moses rises to a higher level; he ventures to put God in mind of what he had himself declared to Moses in the fullest revelation which he had ever made of his own unchangeable character, namely, that of all divine prerogatives, the most divine was that of forgiving sins and showing mercy."—Pulpit Commentary

"But my servant Caleb, because he had another spirit with him, and hath followed me fully, him will I bring into the land whereinto he went; and his seed shall possess it" (vs. 24).

"God here bears a very high testimony to his servant Caleb: and that which gained him this honour from God's mouth, we shall find to be his sincerity, especially in that business when he was sent to search the land of Canaan. He had great temptations then to tell another tale. The Israelites were so sick of their enterprise, that he should be the welcomest messenger that brought the worst news, from which they might have some colour for murmuring against Moses who had brought them into such straits; and of twelve that were sent, there were ten that suited their answer to this discontented humour of the people; so that by making a contrary report to theirs, he did not only come under the suspicion of a liar, but hazard his life among an enraged people; yet such was the courage of this holy man, faithfulness to his trust, and trust in his God, that as he says himself (vs. 7), 'He brought him,' that is, Moses, who had sent him, 'word again, as it was in his heart'; that is, he did not, for fear or favour, accommodate himself; but what in his conscience he thought true, that he spake; and this, because it was such an eminent proof of his sincerity; is called by Moses (vs. 24) 'following God fully, or wholly'; for which the Lord erects such a pillar of remembrance over his head, that shall stand as long as that Scripture itself."—Gurnall

Caleb was:

1. A servant of God
2. A noble man
3. Courageous
4. Believing
5. Self Denying
6. Zealous
7. Obedient to God
8. Persevering in his work

9. Pure in heart and life
10. Constant and steadfast in faith

"*Caleb's integrity*—Consider—I. What groundwork is requisite in a man to enable him to follow the Lord fully. He must—1. Have a principle of saving faith; 2. Esteem God to be the chief good; 3. In all things value God's interest before his own; 4. Be able to die for God. II. What it is to follow the Lord fully. 1. It excludes— (1) Partial obedience; (2) Sinister ends; (3) Lukewarmness; (4) Formality; (5) Fickleness. 2. It includes —(1) Obedience to the whole will of God; (2) Freeness of obedience ; (3) Satisfaction with measure of success; (4) Disregard of men; (5) Disregard of impediments. III. How God rewards those who follow him fully. They shall—1. See and know more of him; 2. Receive more from him."—R. Vines

"*Integrity next to sincerity.*—

Next to sincerity remember still
Thou must resolve upon integrity.
God will have all thou hast—thy mind, thy will,
Thy thoughts, thy words, thy works. A nullity
It proves when God, who should have all, doth find
That there is any one thing left behind."

—G. Herbert

"And Caleb stilled the people before Moses, and said, Let us go up at once, and possess it; for we are well able to overcome it" (Num. 13:30).

"It is very material with what eyes we look upon all objects. Fear doth not more multiply evils, than faith diminishes them; which is therefore bold, because either it sees not, or contemns, that terror which fear represents to the weak. There is none so valiant as the believer."—Bp. Hall

16

THE TEN TEMPTATIONS

(Numbers 14:22-24)

"Because all those men, which have seen my glory, and my miracles, which I did in Egypt, and in the wilderness, and have tempted me now these ten times, and have not hearkened unto my voice; Surely they shall not see the land which I sware unto their fathers, neither shall any of them that provoked me see it; But my servant Caleb, because he had another spirit with him, and hath followed me fully, him will I bring into the land whereinto he went; and his seed shall possess it."

Ten is the number of completeness. Rebekah was entreated to tarry *ten days* before starting from home to meet the bridegroom, the loving Issac (complete delay). Eliezer took with him *ten* camels and bracelets of *ten* shekels as he started from the homeland to seek a bride.

Jacob's wages were changed *ten* times, thus setting forth the complete disappointment of life while away from God and God's land. The tables of stone written by the finger of God contained *ten* commandments (complete law).

The parable of the *ten* pounds and *ten* talents set forth complete stewardship and complete responsibility.

The woman lost one of *ten* pieces of silver and consequently marred the completeness of her betrothal, wedding, and marital happiness.

Christ healed *ten lepers* (complete work), but only *one* returned to give thanks (incomplete work on man's part).

The dragon of Daniel had *ten* horns (complete power).

Daniel and the three Hebrews were proved *ten* days (complete testing), and were *ten* times better than the other college fed students (complete blessing).

"The tithe is the Lord's." The *tenth* is the Lord's and is thus an acknowledgment that all we have, belongs to God.

Israel tempted the Lord *ten* times, setting forth their complete failure and weakness.

The first temptation was at the Red Sea when Israel yielded to *despair.* God performed a miracle on their behalf, delivering Israel and destroying Pharaoh and his hosts.

The second temptation was at Marah when Israel *murmured* because of the bitter waters. God commanded Moses to cast the branch of the tree into the bitter waters, and the waters were made sweet.

The branch (Christ) of the tree (Calvary) cast into our Marahs (bitter experiences) will turn all our bitterness into sweetness.

The third temptation was in the wilderness of

sin. *Hunger* was the cause of the discontent. Israel's *stomachs* got the better of them and, like Esau, they were ready to sell out for a basin of broth. God gave the manna from heaven. In condescending love and grace he rained them bread from heaven.

The fourth temptation was at Sinai. Here the people gave way to *impatience*. Aaron made the golden calf, and Israel fell into idolatry.

The fifth temptation was the wickedness of Nadab and Abidu, who offered strange fire. *Wilfulness* was the crime of these wayward and wicked sons of the high priest. They died because of their sin.

The sixth temptation was at Taberah when again the people *complained*. The Holy Spirit was grieved. The kindness of God was bestowed in vain, and judgment was sent.

The seventh temptation was at Kibroth-hattaavah. *Lusting* after flesh, with their hearts already in Egypt, the people were ready to kill God and also their leader, Moses. The patience of God was being exhausted, and Israel was fast approaching the line beyond which there is neither hope nor mercy.

The eighth temptation was at Rephidim. There was no water and they were *thirsty*. Instead of bowing before God on their knees, they mounted their high horses of vanity and pride and rebellion and blamed God, Moses, and everyone but themselves. God gave them water out of a flinty rock.

The ninth temptation was at Horeb. Israel was wilful and *disobedient.* God's mercy still lingers, but Israel comes nearer and nearer doom.

The tenth temptation was at Kadesh-barnea where their *unbelief* sealed their doom. They crossed the line. God's dove of mercy spread her wings and departed, and Israel perished in the wilderness. Complete failure brought complete judgment.

17

KADESH TO BARNEA

(Numbers, Chapters 15-19)

At Kadesh-barnea, Israel rebelled and refused to go over and possess the land of Canaan. "Let us therefore fear, lest, a promise being left us of entering into his rest, any of you should seem to come short of it" (Heb. 4:1).

That generation of rebels *perished* in the wilderness. "I will therefore put you in remembrance, though ye once knew this, how that the Lord, having saved the people out of the land of Egypt, afterward destroyed them that believed not" (Jude 5).

Forty years later the new generation under Joshua entered the land of rest. "There remaineth therefore a rest to the people of God" (Heb. 4:9). "Let us labour therefore to enter unto that rest, lest any man fall after the same example of unbelief" (Heb. 4:11).

The history of Israel during the years of submergence is full of interest. God did not abandon his people. He supplied them every day with manna. He provided them also with raiment and shoes so that they had the actual necessities of life. "And thou shalt remember all the way which the LORD thy God led thee these forty years in the wilderness, to humble thee, and to prove thee, to know what was in thine heart, whether thou wouldest keep his commandments, or no. And he humbled thee, and suffered thee to hunger, and fed thee with manna, which thou knewest not, neither did thy fathers know; that he might make thee know that man doth not live by bread only, but by every word that proceedeth out of the mouth of the LORD doth man live. Thy raiment waxed not old upon thee, neither did thy foot swell, these forty years. Thou shalt also consider in thine heart, that, as a man chasteneth his son, so the LORD thy God chasteneth thee. Therefore thou shalt keep the commandments of the LORD thy God, to walk in his ways, and to fear him" (Deut. 8:2-6). "And I have led you forty years in the wilderness; your clothes are not waxen old upon you, and thy shoe is not waxen old upon thy foot. Ye have not eaten bread, neither have ye drunk wine or strong drink, that ye might know that I am the LORD your God" (Deut. 29:5-6).

Another glimpse into their religious condition is given us in Joshua 5:2-9, where we learn that the rite of circumcision fell into abeyance. When Joshua and the children of Israel entered Canaan, all the males were circumcised, and thus the reproach was rolled away and the place was called Gilgal. "At that time the LORD said unto Joshua, Make thee sharp knives, and circumcise again the children of Israel the second time, and Joshua made him sharp knives, and circumcised the children of

Israel at the hill of the foreskins. And this is the cause why Joshua did circumcise: All the people that came out of Egypt, that were males, even all the men of war, died in the wilderness by the way, after they came out of Egypt. Now all the people that came out were circumcised; but all the people that were born in the wilderness by the way as they came forth out of Egypt, them they had not circumcised. For the children of Israel walked forty years in the wilderness, till all the people that were men of war, which came out of Egypt, were consumed, because they obeyed not the voice of the LORD; unto whom the LORD sware that he would not shew them the land, which the LORD sware unto their fathers that he would give us, a land that floweth with milk and honey. And their children, whom he raised up in their stead, them Joshua circumcised: for they were uncircumcised, because they had not circumcised them by the way. And it came to pass, when they had done circumcising all the people, that they abode in their places in the camp, till they were whole. And the Lord said unto Joshua, *This day have I rolled away the reproach of Egypt from off you.* Wherefore the name of the place is called Gilgal unto this day" (Joshua 5:2-9).

In Ezekiel we learn that God poured out His fury upon them in the wilderness. Nevertheless his eye spared them from being utterly consumed. "Wherefore I cause them to go forth out of the land of Egypt, and brought them into the wilderness. And I gave them my statutes, and shewed them my judgments, which if a man do, he shall even live in them. Moreover also I gave them my sabbaths, to be a sign between me and them, that they might know that I am the LORD that sanctify them. But the house of Israel rebelled against me in the wilderness; they walked not in my statutes, and they despised my judgments, which if a man do, he shall even live in them; and my sabbaths they greatly polluted: then I said, I would pour out my fury upon them in the wilderness, to consume them. But I wrought for my name's sake, that it should not be polluted before the heathen, in whose sight I brought them out. Yet also I lifted up my hand unto them in the wilderness, that I would not bring them into the land which I had given them, flowing with milk and honey, which is the glory of all lands; because they despised my judgments, and walked not in my statutes, but polluted my sabbaths: for their heart went after their idols. Nevertheless mine eye spared them from destroying them, neither did I make an end of them in the wilderness" (Ezekiel 20:10-17).

While obscurity hangs over the doings of Israel during their forty years of wandering, we are not altogether ignorant of those tragic years of suffering and shame. Israel evidently remembered God and kept up a form of godliness without any manifestation of the divine presence and power. "Have ye offered unto me sacrifices and offerings in the wilderness forty years, O house of Israel?"

Not only was Israel given to idol worship at this time but they also evidently worshipped the host of heaven. Having disobeyed the Creator they worshipped the creation. "Then God turned, and gave them up to worship the host of heaven; as it is written in the book of the prophets, O ye house of Israel, have ye offered to me slain beasts and sacrifices by the space of forty years in the wilderness? Yea, ye took up the tabernacle of Moloch, and the star of your God Remphan, figures which ye made to worship them; and I will carry you away beyond Babylon" (Acts 7:42-43).

These years of wandering in the wilderness ought to warn us against wilfulness in our own days. "It is a fearful thing to fall into the hands of the living God."

18

THE SIN OF GATHERING STICKS

(Numbers 15: 32-36)

32. And while the children of Israel were in the wilderness, they found a man that gathered sticks upon the sabbath day.

33. And they that found him gathering sticks brought him unto Moses and Aaron, and unto all the congregation:

34. And they put him in ward, because it was not declared what should be done to him.

35. And the LORD said unto Moses, The man shall be surely put to death: all the congregation shall stone him with stones without the camp.

36. And all the congregation brought him without the camp, and stoned him with stones, and he died; as the LORD commanded Moses.

"And all the congregation . . . . stone him with stones, and he died . . . ." (vs. 36).

This is not an incident of unimportance or of extreme and intolerable severity. It was a clean case of law violation, wilfulness and wickedness. If this man had been Cain, he would have acted as the carnal and conceited Cain acted. Placed in the same circumstances in which Ishmael found himself, he would have mocked God's holy Isaac just as Ishmael mocked. It is not a question of sticks or days, it is a question of heart attitudes towards God and truth. The man who was stoned for gathering sticks on the Sabbath was as crooked as Cain, as nasty and as haughty as Nimrod, as full of folly as Pharaoh, as carnal as Achan, as bad as the drunken Belshazzar, as sinful and deceitful as Demas and as hateful as Herod. If a man will wilfully and knowingly break one of God's commandments he will break all of God's commands in due time. "He that offendeth in one point is guilty of all." The person who will steal will also tell lies and the man who will tell one lie will steal. It is the principle that matters. It is a question of the state of the soul and not of sticks on the Sabbath.

The man forfeited his life *not* because he gathered sticks but because he sinned against God, sinned against society and sinned against his own soul. He forfeited his life because he violated God's law. The man who would gather sticks on the Sabbath knowing it was contrary to the Word of God would also gather gold rings from the fingers of a corpse in a casket, and take the pennies from the eyes of the dead. We need to learn that law is eternal and impartial. We must not expect the Burlington Zephyr to stop because we choose to step in the tracks of the accelerator. Law pulverizes us as well as protects. Law grinds as well as acting as a guardian.

Law curses the crooked and careless and blesses the believer and lawful. The same sun that softens wax will harden clay. It will bless you with warmth, life, light, and heat but it will also burn and blister you unmercifully. The man who will gather sticks on the Sabbath against God's command, may also blaspheme, steal, swear, drink, rape, murder and indeed break any other command of God. There are no little sins in the sight of God.

Shall we listen to God and obey God? Shall we listen to Satan and please self? Shall we keep the law or become lawless? Shall we follow God and the Bible or shall each man declare for himself his own decalogue? This is the issue. This is the question. God or no God. Law or no law. The Bible or no Bible. The Sabbath or Stalinism. Holiness or Hitlerism. In the last analysis we must all choose between the Sabbath and sticks.

"*The Sabbath-breaker stoned.* The guilt of profaning the Sabbath. It is—1. An unreasonable sin. Consider who it is that requires the observation of the Sabbath; what portion of our time it is that He requires; for whose sake He requires it 2. A presumptuous sin: it is 'a reproaching of God himself' as a hard Master that is unfit to be obeyed. 3. Its danger. This sin is particularly specified as a very principal occasion of bringing down all those judgments with which the Jews were visited at the time of their captivity in Babylon."—Simeon

Sabbath observance. A young man, well off

in the world, and an elderly man of business, were riding in a railway carriage together, between London and a country town, when the question of Sunday amusements came up. "I maintain that Sunday ought to be a general holiday," said the younger, in a tone which betokened assurance and presumption, "and the people ought not to be kept out of such places as the Zoological Gardens and the Crystal Palace grounds. I would have Sunday used for recreation." "Recreation!" answered the elder, gravely, "yes, that is the very word. The Sabbath is meant for recreation, and if people were recreated, they would want very little of the so-called recreation which they now make so much of."

Sabbath is called "Day of light" by the Jews; "day of silence" by the African; "praying day" by the Cree Indians; the early Christians called it the "queen of days."

It is a curious fact that though the rain keeps thousands away from church on Sunday it does not deter a single man from attending to his business on week-days.

"And all the congregation brought him without the camp, and stoned him with stones, and he died; as the LORD commanded Moses" (vs. 36).

"This example was evidently introduced to illustrate the foregoing law. A certain person was observed gathering sticks on the Sabbath day, in contempt of the commandment: and he was condemned, as a presumptuous offender, to be stoned for a warning to the rest; which sentence was executed the next day. May we ever remember this awful story, and take warning by it!"—Scott

19

RIBBAND OF BLUE

(Numbers 15:38-39)

"Speak unto the children of Israel, and bid them that they make them fringes in the borders of their garments throughout their generations, and that they put upon the fringe of the borders a ribband of blue; And it shall be unto you for a fringe, that ye may look upon it, and remember all the commandments of the LORD, and do them; and that ye seek not after your own heart and your own eyes, after which ye use to go a whoring."

Every word of God is inspired and profitable. Blue is the color of the heavens. It is first mentioned in connection with the tabernacle in the wilderness. The curtains of the tabernacle were to be made of blue, purple, scarlet and fine twined linen. The blue color speaks of a heavenly Christ. As the rainbow which God put upon the clouds after the deluge reminded Noah of God's promised mercy, so the blue ribband reminded Israel of their high and holy calling. They were to be a separated, holy, heavenly people. The blue ribband was attached to their every day clothes, reminding them that their walk and talk was to be as becometh a heavenly people. The *rainbow* which God put upon the clouds after the deluge, reminded

Noah of God's promised mercy and the blue *ribband* reminded these Israelites of their obligation to walk before God as becometh a separated and heavenly people. This blue ribband attached to their every day clothing was a constant reminder to them that their daily life was to be clean in the sight of God.

The poor sick woman touched the blue border of Christ's garment and by so touching was made "instantly whole." She touched a heavenly Christ and was healed.

"That ye may remember, and do all my commandments, and be holy unto your God. I am the LORD your God, which brought you out of the land of Egypt, to be your God: I am the LORD your God" (Num. 15:40-41).

"It is remarkable that the modern Jews generally neglect this precept, which they might obey; whilst many parts of their religion are become absolutely impracticable. We should use every means of refreshing our memories, in respect to the precepts of our God, of animating and quickening our obedience, and of arming our minds against temptation."—Scott

A teacher was explaining to her class the words concerning God's angels, "ministers of his who do his pleasure," and asked: "How do the angels carry out God's will?" Many answers followed. One said: "They do it directly." Another: "They do it with all their heart." A third: "They do it well."

And after a pause a quiet little girl added: "They do it without asking any questions."

An officer who had received his orders from the Duke of Wellington, urged the impossibility of executing them. Wellington replied, "I did not ask your opinion; I gave you my orders, and expect them to be obeyed." Implicit obedience is required of every soldier of Christ.

Ours not to reason why;
Ours not to make reply;
Ours but to do or die.

Obedience, Happiness of. It is foolish to strive with what we cannot avoid; we are born subjects, and to obey God is perfect liberty: he that does this, shall be free, safe, and quiet; all his actions shall succeed to his wishes.

—Seneca.

20

KORAH, DATHAN, ABIRAM, ON

(Numbers 16:1-3)

"Now Korah, the son of Izhar, the son of Kohath, the son of Levi, and Dathan and Abiram, the sons of Eliab, and On, the son of Peleth, sons of Reuben, took men: And they rose up before Moses, with certain of the children of Israel, two hundred and fifty princes of the assembly, famous in the congregation, men of renown: And they gathered themselves together against Moses and against Aaron, and said unto them, Ye take too much upon you, seeing all the congregation are holy, every one of them, and the LORD is among them: wherefore then lift ye up yourselves above the congregation of the Lord?"

These words set forth the cruel, determined and sinister conspiracy of the slanderous Korah, Dathan, and devilish company. Their murderous whisperings amongst each other stirred up the flame of envy, jealousy, and spleen in one another's hearts. The sin of these office seekers was more serious because they were "men of renown" and should have shown a better example. Unfortunately it is often men of renown who are the office hunters, who itch to be a member of every committee and who are even so self-centered, egotistical, and conceited as to ask to be placed on different boards. Influential sinners are especially dangerous. Job seekers are generally unjust and unscrupulous. Instead of being a brother and helper to Moses and satisfied with his present position of honour in the assembly and among his brethren Korah went about whispering and underhandedly undermining the God-called leader of the hosts.

Bringing an utterly false charge against Moses "ye take too much upon you" (see vs. 7) which later recoiled upon themselves, they caused a serious division amongst the brethren. Their murmurings and gruntings were not against Moses merely but against the Lord (vs. 11). For inasmuch as ye do it unto the least of these ye do it unto me (Christ).

The friendliness and generosity and manliness of Moses encouraged them in their madness and folly. They became impudent and nasty. (See vss. 13-14.)

The evils which they had brought upon themselves they charged to Moses, the man of God, as such nasty, miserable, and despicable office seekers always do. Their infatuation with themselves and their madness against Moses, the friend of God, brought swift and horrible vengeance from an insulted Deity. New and strange sins call for new and strange scourgings and judgments. The groaning ground refused to bear these godless rebels, the earth opened its mouth and Korah and his conceited companions dropped alive into hell. Enoch and Elijah went to heaven without dying while Korah and company went down to their well-deserved damnation also without dying. God performed a new thing.

"And the earth opened her mouth, and swallowed them up, and their houses, and all the men that appertained unto Korah, and all their goods. They, and all that appertained to them, went down alive into the pit, and the earth closed upon them: and they perished from among the congregation" (Num. 16:32-33).

"So soon as the innocent are severed, the guilty perish: the earth cleaves and swallows up the rebels. This element was not used to such morsels. It devours the carcasses of men; but bodies informed with living souls, never before. To have seen them struck dead upon the earth had been fearful; but to see the earth at once their executioner and grave, was more horrible. Neither the sea nor the earth are fit to give passage; the sea is moist and flowing, and will not be divided for the continuity of it; the earth is dry and massy, and will neither yield naturally, nor meet again when it hath yielded; yet the waters did cleave to give way to Israel, for their preservation; the earth did cleave to give way to the conspirators, in judgment: both sea and earth did shut their jaws again upon the adversaries of God. There was more wonder in this latter. It was a marvel that the waters opened; it was no wonder that they shut again; for the retiring and flowing was natural. It was no less marvel that the earth opened; but more marvel that it shut again; because it had no natural disposition to meet, when it was divided. Now might Israel see, that they had to do with a God that could revenge with ease."—Bishop Hall

"And all Israel that were round about them fled at the cry of them: for they said, Lest the earth swallow us up also" (vs. 34).

"The common people were not so fast gathered to Korah's flattering persuasion before, as now they ran from the sight and fear of his judgment. I marvel not if they could not trust that earth whereon they stood, while they knew their hearts had been false. It is a madness to run away from punishment, and not from sin."—Bishop Hall

"And Aaron took as Moses commanded, and ran into the midst of the congregation; and, behold, the plague was begun among the people: and he put on incense, and made an atonement for the people. And he stood between the dead and the living; and the plague was stayed. Now they that died in the plague were about fourteen thousand and seven hundred, beside them that died about the matter of Korah. And Aaron returned unto Moses unto the door of the tabernacle of the congregation: and the plague was stayed" (vs. 47-50).

"Tragical as is this picture, it bears but a feeble type, and yet how fearful, of a plague that is raging amongst mankind, which is carrying off its thousands every week, not only to the peaceful abodes of the tomb, but to the fearful horrors of a death that never, never dies. Dear reader, you are infected with this plague, and soon, unless it is cured, it will destroy you. This plague is sin; it was introduced into your nature at your birth, and ever since then it has been increasing; and now, unless it has been checked by the grace of God, every faculty and feeling is tainted with it. Your moral condition is well described in these words of the prophet; 'The whole head is sick, and the whole heart faint; from the sole of the feet even unto the head, there is no soundness in you, but wounds, and bruises, and putrifying sores.' Here is your portrait pencilled by the Holy Ghost . . . . This plague is contagious—you carry it wherever you go;it spreads fast, and its effects will be felt throughout eternal ages. Are you aware that you are spreading this disease, and that you are responsible for it? How many immortal souls will be lost by the influence of your example! Ponder this solemn question, and, remember, you are dying; then apply to the 'Balm in Gilead,' to 'the Physician there,' that the health of your soul may be recovered." —H.B.

21

THE RED HEIFER

(Numbers 19:2-10)

1. The pure red heifer was very rare in Palestine and of great price.

2. Very few people have ever seen a pure blooded red heifer.

3. It was to be without spot.

4. No yoke was to have come upon her.

5. The female of the species denotes affection, kindness, and fruitfulness.

6. The heifer was to be taken and slain.

7. It was slain on an altar of wood.

8. The blood of the slain sacrifice was to be sprinkled seven times.

9. The heifer was then to be completely burned in the sight of the high priest.

10. The ashes of the heifer were carefully gathered and laid in a clean place.

The red color reminds of sin which Christ bore in his own body. He was also made *sin* for us. Only a few, a very few, a choice few have ever beheld the beauty, grace and glory of the crucified Christ.

He was without spot, for in him was no sin and

though made sin for us He nevertheless knew no sin.

He was without spot or blemish.

Christ's submission to the law of sin and death was altogether spontaneous and hence no yoke. Yokes are necessary because of sin. He was holy, harmless, and undefiled and separate from sinners.

Christ also was slain and slain outside the camp, and on an altar of wood, the cross.

Perfect atonement and complete cleansing is now possible to all the children of God. The number seven is the number of perfection.

After Christ's death, clean hands carefully laid his body away in a clean place, a new tomb.

The red heifer is one of the most complete types of our Lord Jesus Christ.

Combining the stories of Isaac, and Joseph, in the Book of Genesis, with the Paschal Lamb of Exodus, the offerings of Leviticus, the brazen serpent, cities of refuge and the red heifer of Numbers, we may behold the perfect picture of the Christ of the New Testament.

"Bring thee a red heifer"

In oriental lands the heifer is the servant of man. It pulls the loads of others. It is the the great burden bearer. It stands ready for suffering, service or sacrifice. The heifer speaks of Christ, as the faithful, suffering servant of God and men—Christ the burden bearer, Christ the lifter of loads, Christ the wonderful carrier of the world's cares, Christ, the sufferer to save from sin. The color *red* speaks of the precious blood of our burden bearers, and like the people of God in Old Testament times we bring our red heifer, the Lord Jesus Christ.

"Wherein is no blemish"

This sets forth the *inward* perfection of our Lord Jesus Christ, as the words "without spot" reveal his *outward* perfection. Within and without he was faultless and flawless.

"And upon which never came yoke"

A yoke is put on in order to restrain the wild nature and bring it into subjection. There was therefore no need of a yoke in connection with the Christ of Calvary. Born of the Spirit, filled with the Spirit, and led by the Spirit, he was without that wild nature which is common to man. Submitting himself to God and subjecting himself to the will of God, he did not bear a yoke, for it was unnecessary. Christ never bore the yoke of sin and since all yokes are the result of sin, the red heifer which typified Christ was to be without a yoke.

"Bring her forth without the camp"

This sets forth the rejection of Christ by the religious world of his day. It was the fulfilment of the prophet's words: "He was despised and rejected of men." "Let us go forth *without the camp* bearing his reproach."

"And one shall slay her before his face"

The one, which is in italics, represents the whole race of mankind. The slaying of the red heifer foreshadows the cross.

"Take . . . . and . . . . sprinkles of her blood"

The *take* sets forth the act of faith as the sprinkling sets forth the appropriation and practical sprinkling of the blood of Christ necessary before atonement could be possible.

"Before the tabernacle seven times"

Christ took his blood and sprinkled it on high and thus established a perfect cure for sin. The expression *seven times* assures us that perfect atonement has been made, for seven is the number of perfection.

"And one shall burn the heifer"

The one, which also is in italics, speaks of God, whose anger burned against the Darling of his heart because he was bearing the sin of the world. The wrath of God must spend itself either against the sinner or the substitute. Christ became a willing substitute and God's worth spent itself on the holy head of our spotless substitute, and hence we may go free. "It *pleased Jehovah to bruise him."*

"In a clean place"

"And a man that is clean shall gather up the ashes of the heifer and lay them up without the camp in a clean place." Ashes proved the acceptance of the offering.

The fire of God burned up the victim, and the ashes were a proof of acceptance.

The *ashes* speak of the body of Christ.

The *clean man* sets forth the loving disciples of Christ who took up the body of their Lord.

The *clean place* was a fitting foreshadowing of the new tomb in which the body of Christ was laid.

The heifer was thus:

1. Holy
2. Tested
3. Slain
    a. Its blood was shed.
    b. Its blood was sprinkled.
4. Burnt with fire
5. Ashes buried
    a. By clean hands
    b. In a clean place
6. Atonement accomplished
7. Purification possible

22

MISTAKES OF MOSES

(Number 20:10-12)

10. And Moses and Aaron gathered the congregation together before the rock, and he said unto them, Hear now, ye rebels; must we fetch you water out of this rock.

11. And Moses lifted up his hand, and with his rod he smote the rock twice: and the water came out abundantly, and the congregation drank, and their beasts also.

12. And the LORD spake unto Moses and Aaron, Because ye believed me not, to sanctify me in the eyes of the children of Israel, therefore ye shall not bring this congregation into the land which I have given them.

Numbers 20:7-13 is filled with instruction for believers today. God demands exact obedience to his holy Word and to his revealed will. Any old thing, any old time, any old place will not do. Insertions of our own word, will, and ways always bring down the withering woes of God upon us. Moses was ordered to take "the rod" (vs. 8), which was the rod of Aaron, the branch of intercession, the rod of life, beauty, fruitfulness and flowers and "speak" to the rock. Instead of taking the rod of life and intercession (Christ) he took his own rod, the rod of law, government, order, majesty and rule. Instead of speaking to the "rock" (Christ) he spake to the people and instead of speaking to the rock, he smote it, and smote it *twice.* These mistakes and sins of Moses robbed God of glory and ruined his chances of continued leadership. Taking glory to himself "must we fetch you water," and scolding God's people "ye rebels," with his own "rod" (vs. 11) he smote the rock twice and while the water came out abundantly God was displeased and Moses died outside of the promised land. It is a very serious thing *not* to exactly follow the Word of God.

"The conduct of the great leader on this occasion was hasty and passionate (Ps. 106:33). He had been directed to 'speak' to the rock, but he 'smote it twice' in his impetuosity, thus endangering the blossoms of the rod, and, instead of speaking to the rock, he spoke to the people in a fury."—Jamieson, Fausset and Brown

"Moses and Aaron not to enter Canaan. Learn from this sad history—I. That the best of men are not infallible: they are not precluded, by their goodness, from the possibility of committing sin. II. That with God there is the strictest impartiality. Although Moses was so much 'the friend of God' yet God punished him for sin, as well as others. III. That a seemingly small sin will often be followed by a great punishment."—H. Brett

"*Watch and pray.* A child would generally stand on its feet in a gust of wind if he knew it was coming; but when the wind happens to come around a corner furiously, he may be taken off his feet. Mind you are well ballasted by prayer every morning before your vessel puts out to sea, or carrying the quantity of sail you do, you may be blown out upon the waves to your perpetual shipwreck. Watch constantly against those things which are thought to be no temptations. The most poisonous serpents are found where the sweetest flowers grow, and when Cleopatra would have an asp to poison herself, it was brought in a basket of fair flowers. Beware of arrows shot from a golden bow, or by a woman's hand. 'Watch and pray, that ye enter not into temptation.' "—C. H. Spurgeon

It was but one act, but it blighted the fair flower of a noble life, and shut the soul, from the reward much seemed so nearly within its grasp.

"And the LORD spake unto Moses and Aaron, Because ye believe me not, to sanctify me in the eyes of the children of Israel, therefore ye shall not bring this congregation into the land which I have given them" (Num. 20:12).

"Though the people were rebels, and Moses called them so at times without offence, yet he evidently spake at this time with an angry spirit. He also assumed the honour to himself and Aaron, instead of ascribing it to God: 'Must we fetch you water out of this rock?' He also seems not firmly to have believed that water would be given, and did not think it sufficient simply to speak to the rock, as he was commanded; and he therefore hastily smote it twice. Thus it appears, that they neither properly believed God, nor did Him honour in the sight of the people."—Comp. Bible

"The sin of Moses. I. What there was sinful in Moses. 1. Disobedience to the divine command; 2. Immoderate heat and passion. 3. Unbelief; 4. All this was publicly displayed, and so the more dishonoring to God. II. What we may learn from this story. 1. What a holy and jealous God is ours; 2. The Lord's children need not think it strange if they are much exercised in that grace in which they most excel; 3. Let us not be surprised to see or hear saints failing under such tests; 4. Never think yourselves secure from falling till you are at the end of your race; 5. Learn the need we have to constantly guard our unruly passions; 6. Though God pardons the iniquity of His servants, yet He will take vengeance on their inventions."—T. Boston

"Anger. If anger arises in thy breast, instantly seal up thy lips, and let it not go forth; for like fire when it wants vent, it will suppress itself. It is good in a fever to have a tender and smooth tongue; but is better that it be in anger; for if it be rough and distempered, there it is an ill sign, but here it is an ill cause. Angry passion is a fire, and angry words are like breath to fan them

together; they are like steel and flint, sending out fire by mutual collision."—Jeremy Taylor

Bible examples on anger: Cain (Gen. 4:5-6); Esau (Gen. 27:45); Saul (I Sam. 20:30); Ahab (I Kings 21:4); Naaman (II Kings v. 11); Asa (II Chr. 16:10); Uzziah (II Ch. 24:19); Nebuchadnezzar (Dan. 3:13); Jonah (Jon. 4:4); Herod (Matt. 2:16); Jews (Luke 4:28); High Priest (Acts 5:17; 7:54).

23

DEATH OF AARON

(Numbers 20:22-29)

Aaron was the Mediator between God and man, a fitting type of Christ. The rod, or dry stick, or branch of a tree which blossomed and budded overnight was also a fitting foreshadowing of Christ in resurrection power, glory, and fruitfulness. Life, fruit, and flowers overnight was a most convincing proof of divinity and a proper emblem of the coming resurrection of Christ. A dead branch restored to vegetable life, fruitfulness, and usefulness was indeed a miracle of miracles. The Branch of Jehovah (Christ) was and is the miracle of miracles. It was a branch that was plunged into the bitter waters of Marah and which turned the bitternesses into sweetnesses. It was the branch that smote the rock and the flint rock gave forth its refreshing water. Both the "branch" and the "rock" like "Abel" and his "lamb" were foreshadowings of our Lord and Saviour Jesus Christ.

The "rod" of Moses represents and speaks of Christ in righteous government working for the benefit and blessing of his people, while the "rod" of Moses typifies Christ in his atoning and intercessory work for his saints. It was the using of the wrong "rod" that brought trouble to Moses when he smote the rock twice, for in the first place Christ was to be smitten but once and in the second place the "rod" to be used was the intercession rod and not the rod which represented law, order, and government.

1. Aaron means "enlightener." Moses was a type of Christ as prophet, law giver, leader, captain, and shepherd, while Aaron was a type of Christ as priest, intercessor, and mediator. Christ was the light which lighteth every man. "Awake thou that sleepest, and arise from the dead, and Christ shall give thee light."
2. Chosen of God.
3. Had charge of all the holy things.
4. Especially anointed. As Aaron was anointed in a special way, so Christ was anointed by the seven fold Spirit and after his anointing went forth to preach, teach and heal. Chosen by God and having charge of all holy things, Christ was anointed by the Holy Spirit and performed all his works in the power of the Spirit.
5. Clothed with special garments. The garments of glory and beauty worn by Aaron as high priest set forth the beauty and glory of Christ, now in the heavens where he ever liveth to make intercession for us. These garments were laid aside at His birth and taken up again after his resurrection.
6. Aaron had many servants. As Aaron typified

Christ, so the Levites set forth the ministry of believers, who are set apart to serve in the holy things of God. The High Priest typified Christ as our present high priest. The priests who were *sons* of Aaron typify believers who are priests of God. The Levites of the Old Testament typify the separated, consecrated, and sanctified ministry of pastors, teachers, and evangelists of the New Testament.

7. Aaron knew he was to die in a special way.
8. No sickness preceded his death.
9. He neither murmured nor complained.
10. He made atonement for all God's people.

This and more is all true of our Lord Jesus Christ. This Aaron prefigured Christ as priest, Melchisedek typified him as priest king, and Moses typified him as prophet and shepherd.

Aaron's death shows: I. The common destiny of man. II. The rigorousness of moral law. III. The termination of life in the midst of labor. IV. God's agency in man's dissolution. V. The promptitude with which Providence supplies the places of the dead. VI. The trial of human friendships. VII. The painful recognition by society of its greatest losses.

"The removal of a devoted servant of God (*vss.* 25-29). In this death there were: I. The express appointment and arrangement of God. The departure of God's servants is never accidental or un-

foreseen. II. The last attentions and ministrations of pious friendship. Such ministrations and attentions are a privilege to: 1. Those about to depart. 2. Those who for a season are to survive. III. The tokens of Divine favor. In one respect Aaron's death was a sign of Divine displeasure, but this displeasure was only partial. He was allowed to go to the place of his death in his robes of office. IV. The pledge of perpetuity to the divine cause. A successor was immediately, authoritatively, and unquestionably secured to the office that Aaron held. V. The prospect of immortal happiness. Mount Hor was near enough to permit a vision of Canaan." —J. Parsons

"Like birds whose beauties languish, half-concealed
Till mounted on the wing, their glossy plumes
Expanded, shine with azure, green and gold;
How blessings brighten as they take their flight!"

—Young

"It so falls out
That what we have a prize not to the worth,
Whiles we enjoy it; but being lack'd and lost,
Why then we rack the value; then we find
The virtue that possession would not show us
Whiles it was ours."

—Shakespeare

"The discouragements of pious men. I. Some discouragements that the Christian meets with,

though he is in the way to heaven. 1. The way is circuitous; 2. It is through a wilderness; it has no natural tendency to nourish spiritual life; it has much intricacy; 3. It lies through a hostile country; 4. The false steps that are taken are discouraging; 5. The total defection of some from the way; 6. Then length of the way. II. Some considerations to remove discouragement. 1. It is the right way; 2. God is with His people in it; 3. There is no other way that leads to heaven."—R. Hall.

24

THE SERPENT OF BRASS

(Numbers 21)

I. Moses, Type of Christ.

1. A prophet, priest, king, kinsman
2. Born of poor humble parents
3. Member of an oppressed race
4. Saved from death while a babe
5. Unselfish
6. Forsook a palace and riches
7. Meekest man on earth
8. Zealous for God
9. Rejected by his own
10. Married a Gentile bride
11. Died
12. Was buried
13. Was resurrected
14. Before his death he promised *another* leader, i.e., Joshua.
15. His work began with a terrific conflict.
16. He gave up *all* for *others*.

II. The Serpent of Brass

1. Uplifted
2. God planned
3. An act of mercy and grace
4. Saved all who believed

5. Was a *free* remedy
6. Universal (for all) (whosoever)
7. Easy and simple (look and live)

III. The people

1. Undeserving
2. Rebellious
3. Stubborn
4. Poisoned by the serpent
5. Miserable and dying
6. Helpless
7. Hopeless

The serpent and also the goat set forth Christ, who was *made* sin for us, and who was *cursed* in order that we might be blessed.

In the Bodlein library, at Oxford, England, there is a picture setting forth the story of Moses and the brazen serpent. In the picture may be seen a man kneeling and looking at Moses. He continues to writhe in pain. Another may be seen lying on the ground, a serpent at his ear is whispering words of comfort and consolation while the poor dupe is slowly but surely dying of the snake bite. Another may be seen busy binding up the wounds of a friend, ignorant of the fact that both are dying. Another man is fighting the serpent in his own strength, apparently believing in salvation by will power, human strength, and struggle. Moses is prominent in the picture, and back of him there is a man with a calm peaceful countenance. His arms are crossed and he is looking at the serpent and is *healed.* He had been poisoned by the serpent just like the others, but instead of looking at Moses, he looks at the uplifted pole, and *he lives.* The picture speaks for itself.

In this emblem of the brazen serpent is concealed something of the history of sin.

I. It is imparted from without

A serpent-bite is painful and deadly in its effects, so sin is mortal.

II. Also something of the history of redemption

The cross displays the heinousness of sin.

The remedy is necessary, which is coextensive with the evil.

III. Also something of the method of salvation

It is salvation by looking

To look to Christ is indispensable, and fully efficacious.

What a joyful sound, "Look and Live!"

25

DISCOURAGEMENTS

(Numbers 21:4)

Discouragement is one step short of despair and is a subtle trick of the devil.

In studying a foreign language, in seeking to master some scientific subject, in attempting to walk the straight and narrow way, a point of discouragement is reached. Is it worth while to go on and go through? Why not give up and go back? Egypt seems closer than Elim. Leeks and onions smell stronger than milk and honey. Garlic and cucumbers are easier to obtain than the good corn of Canaan, or the sweet grapes of Eschol. We are liable to forget that the holy and right way is always uphill, that mountains strengthen the links, that exercise helps the lungs, and that hard work toughens and tones up the whole system.

Any jellyfish or softshell crab can sail down stream. The temples are all on the hilltops. The cities in which health may be preserved are not in the valleys. The lower levels breed mosquitoes and malaria, and are filled with thickening consumption inviting fogs.

Many discouragements are purely human and physical, but Satan will not slacken his effort on that account. Physical energy may become utterly exhausted and spiritual strength consequently impaired. Even a Samson needs to relax and rest and retire for a season. An Elijah may need a divine Elixir to revive his heart and strengthen his soul. Angels once ministered to our Lord and Saviour Jesus Christ. He once sat weary beside a well. He once was so tired he slept thru a severe storm, and became so hungry that Satan attempted to swallow him up and kill him before the time.

Side by side with your reasons for discouragements, write out a few reasons for rejoicing. Thank God for life, for an open Bible, for the privilege of prayer, for bread to eat and water to drink, for an altar of mercy and the possibility of forgiveness and cleansing from all sin, for hope of heaven when life is over and discouragements and death are destroyed. Side by side with your woes place your wealth and watch Satan "skidaddle." Side by side with your fiery trials and tests place the fulness of divine love and watch Satan flee.

Your discouragements are real, surely! Then make your encouragements real and watch the results. Like Paul, you will shake the viper into the fire, like Daniel you will pass unscathed through the den of your discouragements, and like the three Hebrews you will come out of the fire without even the smell of burning upon you.

26

SINGING AND DIGGING

(Numbers 21:17)

Numbers 21 is filled with delightful truth for our own day. Travelling from Egypt to Canaan the people of God were called upon to pass through some very strange and trying experiences. In special ways, open only to God himself, he marvellously met every need. There was nothing around to satisfy either the hunger or thirst of the Israelites. There is nothing in this world that can satisfy the soul. Unless a supply is sent from above, the people of God must ever remain hungry and thirsty.

In this suggestive chapter we have *a well in a desert*. It was a well obtained by singing and digging, and the digging was done by sticks or staves. The well was digged with staves by divine direction. The lessons for us are simple but sublime. The Rock (Christ) has been smitten. We may now obtain the water of life by simply speaking to the Rock (prayer), and singing to the Rock (faith), and by digging (going down). The full price must be paid, we must go according to divine instruction and direction and all our need will be graciously supplied even in this desert world. The fulness and freeness of salvation is ours if we will sing and dig according to the direction of the lawgiver.

The staves were proof that they were pilgrims, they were going on farther, they were on a journey. Ask and it shall be given, seek and ye shall find, knock and it shall be opened. A well in a wilderness may be yours.

In Exodus 15, God told Moses to *smite* the rock, and it would give forth its water. Moses obeyed, and from the smitten side of the rock there gushed forth waters sufficient to satisfy the need of a thirsty people.

In numbers 20 God told Moses to *speak* to the rock and it would give forth its refreshing water. Instead of *speaking* to the rock as God commanded, Moses became angry, and in *smitting* the rock twice and speaking to the people, Moses grieved the Spirit, spoiled one of God's types, and was prohibited from entering the promised land as a punishment for his rash act and angry words. The rock had already been smitten once, thus foreshadowing the death of Christ on Calvary. In order to obtain water it needed only a word of prayer directed to the rock, and it would have given an abundant supply. "Ask and ye shall receive." The Rock of Ages had already been smitten and "if ye being evil know how to give good gifts to your children, how much more . . . . give the Holy Spirit to them that *ask* him."

In Numbers 21:17-18 you may read, "Then Israel sang this song, Spring up, O well; sing ye unto it; the princes digged the well, the nobles of the people digged it, by the direction of the lawgiver, with their staves." Notice three things:

1. Israel sang.
2. The princes digged.
3. The people delved. (A.R.V.)

The *smiting* of the Rock in Exodus 15 speaks to us of Calvary where the Rock of Ages was smitten. He was to be smitten once and only once.

The *speaking* to the rock of Numbers 20 deals with our regeneration as a consequence or outcome of the Rock having already been smitten.

The singing and digging and delving shows us the way into the Holy of Holies of perfect love. We must dig and dig deep, and while digging we manifest our faith and anticipation by singing, and if we keep digging and singing and singing and digging long enough, we shall strike an artesian well of Holy Ghost, pentecostal salvation.

Rev. Charles G. Finney says: "To me it seems very manifest that the great difference in ministers, in regard to their spiritual influence and usefulness, does not lie so much in their literary and scientific attainments as in the measure of the Holy Ghost which they enjoy.

"A thousand times as much stress ought to be laid upon this part of a thorough preparation for the ministry as has been. Until it is felt, acknowledged, and proclaimed upon the housetops, rung through our halls of science, and sounded forth in our theological seminaries, that this is altogether an indispensable part of the preparation for the work of the ministry, we talk in vain and at random when we talk of the necessity of a thorough preparation and course of training.

"I must confess that I am alarmed, grieved, and distressed beyond expression, when *so much stress* is laid upon the necessity of mere human learning, and so *little* upon the necessity of the *baptism* of the *Holy Ghost.*

"Of what use would ten thousand ministers be without being baptized with the Holy Ghost? Ten thousand times ten thousand of them would be instrumental neither in *sanctifying* the Church nor in *converting* the world."—*Letter in Oberlin Evangelist.*

Bishop Hedding says, in his address to the N. J. Conference: "It is as important that you (ministers) should experience this holy work, as it is that the sinners to whom you preach should be converted."

4. Dr. Adam Clarke says: "If the Methodists give up preaching entire sanctification they will soon lose their glory. . . . This fitness, then, to appear before God, and thorough preparation for eternal glory, *is what I plead for, pray for, and heartily recommend to all true believers,* under the name of Christian *perfection.*"

"Let all those who retain the apostolic doctrine, that the blood of Christ cleanseth from all sin in this life, *press every believer* to go on to perfection, and expect to be saved, while here below, into the fullness of the blessing of the gospel of Christ."—*Theology,* p. 201

5. Bishop Peck says: "The duty of ministers is plain: to set the whole work of grace upon the heart, constantly and plainly, before the people; . . . . to hold out, with the clearness of light, to the Israel of God, everywhere, the glorious privilege of *perfect love,* and *urge* it; not as all the gospel, but the grand result sought in the gospel; not merely as a privilege and a probability, but as a *duty,* as an attainment, which we are in danger of missing, and which is indispensable to our ultimate preservation in the favor of God, and our introduction into heaven."—*Central Idea,* p. 66

6. Bishop Foster says: "Let the pulpit *experience* and teach this glorious privilege as it deserves to be taught, and great evil will be obviated." —*Christian Purity,* p. 277.

7. Dr. Stephen Olin writes: "I trust the day is near when our church will bear a clearer *testimony* on this subject. *It was the peculiarity of early Methodism.* . . . I do not for a moment allow myself to doubt that the great plan of redemption provides for a perfect work here below. I can take no view of the gospel which tolerates lower views. *I can not* PREACH *the gospel in any other light.*"

8. Bishop Asbury wrote to the Rev. Henry Smith, and closed his letter as follows: "Night comes on, and I will close with saying, '*Preach sanc-*

tification, directly and indirectly, in every sermon.'" He wrote to another, "O purity! O Christian perfection! O sanctification! It is heaven below to feel all sin removed. *Preach it,* whether they will hear or forbear. PREACH IT."

9. Bishop McKendree wrote the following to the eloquent Summerfield: "But superior to all these, I trust you will ever keep in view, in *all your ministrations,* the great design which we believe God intended to accomplish in the world, in making us a 'people that were not a people,'—I mean the knowledge, not only of a *free* and a *present,* but also a *full salvation;* in other words, a salvation *from all sin* unto *all holiness.*"

"INSIST MUCH ON THIS; build up the churches *herein,* and *proclaim aloud,* that 'without holiness no man shall see the Lord'; under the guidance of the *Spirit of holiness,* this doctrine will be acknowledged of God: 'signs will follow them that believe' and press after this uttermost salvation, and our people will bear the mark of their high calling— become a holy nation, a peculiar people."

27

THE ERROR OF BALAAM

(Numbers 22-24)

In this story we have some of the most profound and most subtle, as well as some of the most practical religious teachings of the Old Testament.

Balaam undoubtedly had a true knowledge of God. It was not merely the God of nature whom he knew, but Jehovah, the God of grace and the God of Israel. He seemed to know as much about God as either Abraham or Job. Balaam also had an unquestioning faith in God. He had, in a measure, learned to walk by faith and not by sight. God, the will of God, the power of God and the purposes of God were all realities of Balaam. Balaam also was endowed with the prophetic gift. He held a very high official position in the service of God. He knew God. He believed God and desired to obey God.

Balaam's heart, however, was tainted by covetousness. He "loved the ways of unrighteousness." In order to make money he became the hireling of Balak. He was a hireling prophet. Balak was afraid of Israel. The Israelites had conquered the Amorites. Balak was also afraid of God. He attributed the victories of Israel to the power and presence of God. Balak believed in Balaam. He was superstitious enough to believe that Balaam's benediction and malediction were efficacious. He believed that Balaam could blight that which God had blessed. Balak was a diplomat and a psychologist. By means of flatteries, gifts, promises, and rewards, he sought the allegiance of the prophet. He believed that Balaam had his price. Balaam fell into the trap. Balaam became emmeshed in the net so insidiously set for his feet. His love of money cost him his manhood. His thirst for silver cost him his soul. The desire for gold robbed him of glory eternal. Balaam was forbidden to go, and, if he had loved righteousness as much as he lusted for reward, he would have been saved the sorrow and shame of a backslider's grave. A disappointment of God and a grief to the dumb ass, he died in disgrace. "Woe unto them! for they have gone in the way of Cain, and ran greedily after the error of Balaam for reward, and perished in the gainsaying of Core" (Jude 11).

A man may be an eloquent preacher and an imposter at the same time.

"Many shall say unto me, "Lord, Lord, have we not prophesied in thy name?" Better, by far, to be a dumb ass preaching the truth than a Balaam deceiving and being deceived.

A man may have a knowledge of God, desire to do right, and even make known God's truth to others and in the end become a castaway.

Balaam is a type of preacher who primes his pulpit to please the pew. He wanted to please Balak in order to get Balak's gold. He failed to remember that it is impossible to serve God and mammon. He ignored the principles that "no man can serve two masters." Balaam's offspring are not all dead. We have his tribe always with us. Some are in the pulpit while others are in the pew.

"And Balak sent yet again prices, more, and more honourable than they. And they came to Balaam, and said to him, Thus saith Balak the son of Zippor, Let nothing, I pray thee, hinder thee from coming unto me: For I will promote thee unto very great honour, and I will do whatsoever thou sayest unto me: come therefore, I pray thee, curse me this people. And Balaam answered and said unto the servants of Balak, if Balak would give me his house full of silver and gold, I cannot go beyond the word of the LORD my God, to do less or more" (Numbers 22:15-18).

"How near truth and falsehood can lodge together! Here was piety in the lips, and covetousness in the heart. Who can any more regard good words, that hears Balaam speak so like a saint? A house full of gold and silver may not pervert his tongue; his heart is won with less: for if he had not already swallowed the reward, and found it sweet, why did he again solicit God in that which was peremptorily denied him? If his mind had not been bribed already, why did he stay the messengers? Why did he expect a change in God? Why was he willing to feed them with hope of success, who had fed him with hope of recompense? One prohibition is enough for a good man."—Bishop Hall

"Now therefore, I pray you, tarry ye also here this night, that I may know what the Lord will say unto me more. And God came unto Balaam at night, and said unto him, If the men come to call thee, rise up, and go with them; but yet the word which I shall say unto thee, that shalt thou do. And Balaam rose up in the morning, and saddled his ass, and went with the princes of Moab" (Numbers 22:19-21).

"After the peremptory answer which God had given Balaam, he should have spoken to this effect: 'Say no more to me on this subject, but return home, and make the best terms you can with Israel. They are the people of the true God, whom He is determined to bless; and you can do nothing against them, by stratagem or by power, human or Divine; for my part, I cannot, I dare not, and I would not for the world, presume to oppose them; so tempt me no more.' "—Scott

"The state of Balaam's mind was this: He wanted to do what he knew to be very wicked, and contrary to the express command of God; he had inward checks and restraints, which he could not entirely get over; he therefore cast about for ways to reconcile this wickedness to his duty. How great a paradox soever this may appear, as it is indeed a contradiction in terms, it is the very account which the Scripture gives of him."—Bishop Butler

"And God's anger was kindled because he went: and the angel of the LORD stood in the way for an adversary against him. Now he was riding upon his ass, and his two servants were with him. And the ass saw the angel of the LORD standing in the way, and his sword drawn in his hand: and the ass turned aside out of the way, and went into the field: and Balaam smote the ass, to turn her into the way. And when the ass saw the angel of the LORD, she thrust herself unto the wall, and crushed Balaam's foot against the wall: and he smote her again" (Numbers 22:22, 23, 25).

"It was happy for perverse sinners, if they could learn of this beast to run away from foreseen judgment. The revenging angel stands before us; and though we know we shall as certainly die as sin, yet we have not the wit or grace to give back; though it be with the hurt of a foot, to save the body; with the pain of the body, to save the soul."—Bishop Hall

"And the angel of the LORD went further, and stood in a narrow place, where was no way to turn either to the right hand or to the left. And when the ass saw the angel of the LORD, she fell down under Balaam: and Balaam's anger was kindled, and he smote the ass with a staff. And the LORD opened the mouth of the ass, and she said unto Balaam, What have I done unto thee, that thou hast smitten me these three times? And Balaam said unto the ass, Because thou hast mocked me: I would there were a sword in mine hand, for now would I kill thee. And the ass said unto Balaam, Am not I thine ass, upon which thou hast ridden ever since I was thine unto this day? was I ever wont to do so unto thee? And he said, Nay" (Numbers 22:26-30).

"To hear a voice come from that mouth, which was used only to bray, was strange and uncouth; but to hear a beast, whose nature is noted for incapacity, outreason his master, a professed prophet, is the very height of miracles."—Bishop Hall

"But as if no new thing had happened, Balaam returns words to the beast, full of anger, void of admiration. He does not seem to have been at all surprised at the unusualness of the event. Some men make nothing of those things, which overcome others with horror and amazement."—Ibid

"He that put words into the mouth of the ass, puts words into the mouth of Balaam: the words do but pass from him; they are not polluted, because they are not his: as the trunk, through which a man speaks, is not more eloquent for the speech that is uttered through it. What a notable proclamation had the infidels wanted of God's favour to His people, if Balaam's tongue had not been used! How many will once say, 'Lord, we have prophesied in thy name,' who shall hear, 'Verily, I know you not!' "—Bishop Hall

"And he took up his parable, and said, Balak the king of Moab hath brought me from Aram, out of the mountains of the east, saying, Come, curse me Jacob, and come, defy Israel. How shall I curse, whom God hath not cursed? or how shall I defy, whom the LORD hath not defied? For from the top of the rocks I see him, and from the hills I behold him: lo, the people shall dwell alone, and shall not be reckoned among the nations" (Numbers 23:7-9).

" 'Lo, the people,'—This prophecy has been literally fulfilled through a period of 3,300 years to the present day. For notwithstanding their captivities and dispersions through every country on the face of the globe, the Jews still 'dwell alone, and are not reckoned among the nations';—they have been preserved from being confounded with their conquerors and oppressors in foreign lands, in a manner absolutely unprecedented in the annals of the world."—Comp. Bible

"Mark, my soul, the character of God's Israel, and remember, that they are the same in all ages. Distinguishing mercies are sweet mercies. God's people dwell alone, in the everlasting appointment of the Father, by whom they were set apart, and formed for His glory, and given to His Son. They dwell alone, in being brought into the church of Jesus, as the redeemed and purchased by His blood.

They dwell alone, under the sweet influences of the Spirit, by whom they are known, distinguished, regenerated, and sealed unto the day of redemption. Thus set apart, thus formed, thus given, thus redeemed, thus purchased, thus sealed, surely they are not reckoned among the nations, but are supposed to show forth God's praises, who hath called them out of darkness into His marvellous light. My soul! what saith thy experience to these things? O, how different the state, the circumstances, the new birth, the fellowship, pursuits, way, life, and work of God's people from the world! Blessed Jesus! cause me to dwell alone from the nation around; but let me not dwell for a moment without thee; but do thou come with thy Father and the Holy Spirit, according to thy sweet promises, and make constant abode with me!"—Dr. Hawker

"Who can count the dust of Jacob, and the number of the fourth part of Israel? Let me die the death of the righteous, and let my last end be like his!" (Numbers 23:10).

"Bishop Warburton says, had the apostate prophet said, Let me live the life of the righteous, it would have had a much fairer claim. It was a good remark once made on this text, that all mankind have a desire after happiness, and the reward of virtue; but few have resolution to withstand the temptations of vice, and maintain their integrity against the allurements of worldly honours, riches, or sensual pleasures. Just so, says Epictetus, many would be conquerors at the Olympic games, many philosophers like Socrates, though they had no inclination to submit the previous and necessary steps. He that would win the crown must contend." —Old Bible

" 'Oh, let me die his death!' all nature cries;
'Then live his life,'—all nature falters here."
—Young

"It is observed amongst the Papists, that many cardinals, and other great ones, who would think their cowl and religious habit ill becoming them in their health, are yet very ambitious to die and be buried in them, as commonly they are. Though this be a foppery in itself, yet it helps us to a notion of considerable importance. They who live wickedly and loosely, yet like a religious habit very well when they are going into another world. As the young gallant once said to his swaggering companion, after they had visited Ambrose lying on his death-bed, and seen how comfortably he lay triumphing over death as it was approaching: 'O that I might live with thee, and die with Ambrose!' Vain wish! would'st thou, O man, not reap what thou sowest, and find what thou layest up with thy own hands? Dost thou sow cockle, and would'st thou reap wheat? Dost thou fill thy chest with dirt, and expect to find gold when thou openest it? Cheat and gull thyself thou mayest, but thou canst not mock God, who will pay thee in the same coin, at thy death, which thou treasurest up in thy life?"—Gurnall

The doom of the double-hearted—I. He wanted to serve two masters. These were the same as the Lord in after days designated God and mammon. He wanted not to offend either; to please both. He was like Issachar crouching between two burdens. Such is the certain failure of all who make the like attempt. He wanted to earn two kinds of wages. The wages of righteousness and the wages of unrighteousness (II Pet. 2:15), were both in his eyes. III. He wanted to do two opposite things at the same time. He wished both to bless and to curse. He was willing to do either according as it might serve his interests. The only question with him was, "Would it pay?" IV. He wanted two kinds of friendship. V. He wanted to have two religions.

"Balaam belonged to that still numerous class who theoretically know God, and who actually do fear him—but the love and fear of whom are not the governing and regulating principles of their minds. They are convinced, but not converted. They can prize and strongly desire the privileges of God's elect—they long to 'die the death of the righteous,' but are unwilling to live their life. They would serve God; but they must serve mammon also; and in the strife between the two contending influences, their lives are made bitter and their deaths perilous."—Kitto

28

SECOND NUMBERING

(Numbers 26)

The 26th chapter of the book of Numbers is one of those tiresome chapters which is often passed over as unimportant. Like the fifth chapter of Genesis it is largely neglected. Numbers twenty six contains seventy verses and deals exclusively with the offerings of God's people.

The inspired penman records such minor and apparently uninteresting details as the giving of a silver spoon. This chapter, however, is a part of the Word of our wise God. It is profitable for doctrine, reproof, and righteousness. It is written for our learning and instruction.

The God of the Bible is a good and gracious God. He is pleased when his people obey him and vexed when his people become stubborn and perverse. He carefully records and remembers even the smallest gift and the seemingly unimportant and insignificant offering of a spoon. God is concerned about the heart of the giver and not the amount of the gift.

The widow with her two mites gave more than all others for she gave her all. God takes notice of the dimes, nickles, and pennies. He records the amount and remembers the donor. God is interested in the minute details of our daily lives. Our every day worship and our manifestation of love is his daily delight. God remembers and records the name of the giver and the amount of the gift. May we draw your attention to the living and abiding lessons of this lengthy chapter (Numbers 26).

1. *"Take the sum of the children of Israel"*

The chapter deals with the twelve tribes. After 38 years of miracles and warfare they are fewer and weaker than when they started. There are not wanting in every church those who had more zeal eight years ago than they have to day. There are others who know that they had more fire and power and earnestness eighteen years ago than to day. How about it? Have you cooled off? Have you become lukewarm and careless in the things of God? God has a record. He knows your name, your past, and your present. Do you love the prayer meeting as you did twenty-eight years ago? Are you as interested in the salvation of boys and girls and men and women as you were twenty-eight years ago? Better be honest with God and your own heart. A lukewarm state of soul is a dangerous state. The fact that you are not cold and dead and formal may contribute to your being fooled, although you may not have heat enough in you to generate sufficient steam to say "Amen," or to get out to church on Sunday evenings, or Sunday school and prayer meetings. Remember that you are no stronger than your weakest part. Your weakest spot is your strongest spot. "Take the sum of the children of Israel." Make sure of your present standing. Find out where you are. Your past experience does not determine your present standing. Get your bearings today. Before a ship takes to the open sea, she always takes her bearings to make sure that the compass and everything is in order. Better make sure of your present position. To borrow a business term, better take stock. An inventory is in order.

Are you as personally devoted to Christ today as you were in your yesterdays? Are you as interested in his cause and kingdom? Or has someone else or something else run off with your heart's affections? Is Christ crowded out? No room or not quite as much room? Take stock. Get your bearings. Have an inventory. Make sure. Be sure you are heading in the right direction and be sure that you are making progress. Honestly now, do you love the Bible to day? Do you enjoy the prayer meetings to day? Do you love the house of God to day? Are you faithful with your tithes and consistent with your offerings and gifts? Do you surround seekers who want God and help to pray them through? Or do you grab your hat and pocket book and make for the first talkative person in the congregation and then rush home for midnight lunch?

2. *"All that are able to go forth to war"*

These people were preparing to enter Canaan. Canaan was to be a place of rest, quietness, and contentment. To obtain and maintain their promised possession, however, meant conflict and conquest. It is the same today. Sanctification makes us good soldiers. War begins as soon as a person is pardoned and purified and takes up his cross for Christ and the cause of holiness—war in the business world, war in the home, and some times war in the church of which we are members. We are ashamed that it should be so. To testify that we are saved and sanctified starts trouble. The witness to the wondrous grace of full salvation involves war. To confess that Christ has cleansed the heart from all sin starts the conflict. Friends will misunderstand, cousins will criticize, and loved ones will conclude that lunacy and not perfect love is our lot. War will be waged. Hear me! When you get sanctified wholly, prepare for war. Chocolate soldiers will melt away when the heat is turned on. Fireside soldiers will be conspicuous by their absence in a pre-revival campaign. Are you a soldier or a sissy?

The tribe of Reuben was 46,500 strong. After thirty-eight years there were only 43,750. Reuben was weaker at the end than at the beginning. What caused this serious loss?

(1) They lusted after the food of *Egypt.*

Modernizing this truth, we would say that

they went to the movies once a week, neglected prayer and prayer meetings, stayed at home Sunday evenings and listened to Rev. John Doe preach a soothing syrup sermonette. They began to backslide. The Shrine circus, national and international fairs and festivals will rob you of your strength. I warn you against the encroachments of this present evil age.

(2) They murmured under trials.

The children of Israel needed water and, instead of asking God about it, Reuben murmured and complained. Listen, you cannot grow in grace and grunt at the same time. Do not pout under pressure. Walk in the light as God gives you light and all your Jericho walls will crumble. Obey God and watch him give the lions the lockjaw. Mind God and your fiery furnace will disclose to you the presence of the *fourth* in the midst of the flames. Confess Christ and the heavy cross which may now be yours shall suddenly become the conqueror's crown.

Reuben lusted after the food of Egypt, murmured under trials, took the line of least resistance, and was otherwise wasted and weakened by disobedience and wilfulness.

29

ON THE WAY TO CANAAN

(Numbers 33:1-16)

The 33rd chapter of the Book of Numbers is one of those chapters seldom, if ever, read either in private or in public. To most people it is an unpalatable chapter of uninteresting names which are difficult to pronounce and impossible to remember.

Forty-five verses set forth the names of the places from which the Israelites removed and to which they journeyed and in which they pitched their tents.

"They departed—they pitched—they removed they departed—they took their journey—they removed—they departed—and encamped—they removed and pitched" (see vss. 3-49).

The names include, Rameses, Succoth, Etham, Pihahiroth, Migdol, Marah, Elim, Sin, Dophkah, Alush, Rephidim, Sinai, Kibroth-hattaavah, and even Dibon-gad.

It is impossible to go through the chapter without the help of a dictionary. It is considered unimportant and unnecessary and uninteresting.

"All scripture . . . . is profitable." Numbers 33 is part of the Scriptures and hence is profitable. In fact it is not only profitable but it is mighty interesting and instructive.

The 33rd chapter of the Book of Numbers contains a perfect description of the Christian life from its beginning to its end.

1. "These are the *journeys* of the children of Israel" (33:1).

   The people of God are supposed to be journeying and not standing still or going around in circles. Many start out fully intending to go places but something happens on the road and their journeyings cease.

   "Ye did run well, what hath hindered you?" To simply mark time is not to be journeying. We should make daily progress in the things which are pure and peaceable.

   We must check up on ourselves, our Bible reading, family devotions, prayer life, and not forget the assembling of ourselves together as is the manner of some. How about our concern for the salvation of others? Have we been robbed of our power in testimony? Has some one or something stolen our affections from Christ and holiness? Has our love cooled? Have we become lukewarm or is our heart hot with the perfect love of God? "These are the journeyings of . . . ."

2. "Which went forth out of Egypt"

   The word Egypt is a familiar word. It means to *bind,* to bind up, or tie up. Egypt is typical of this present evil world which seeks to bind the people of God. This world is no friend to grace or to God. It has always clubbed its Abels, mocked its Isaacs, beheaded its Johns, imprisoned its Paul's and crucified its Saviour. "Get thee out." "Come out . . . . be separate." "These are the journeyings of the children of Israel which went forth out of Egypt."

3. "With their armies"

God's people are not only a peculiar, pardoned and purified people, but they are a fighting people. They wrestle not against flesh and blood but they are nevertheless soldiers, wielding the sword of the Spirit. Children may need entertainment but warriors are different.

4. "Under the hand of Moses"

An army is not composed of rugged individualists each determined to go his own way and do his own will. If progress is to be made in this war against the forces of sin and Satan, we must fight, march, pull and push together, for in unity there is strength. There must be leaders and leadership. The Israelites went forward *under* the hand of Moses. Like a mighty army the church of God should move and march.

30

RIGHTEOUSNESS OF GOD

(Numbers 33:50-56)

1. The land belonged to God.

   A recognition of the truth that "the earth is the Lord's and the fulness thereof" would solve many social, domestic, and political problems. It would put an end to the proud boast of one nation about our motherland and another nation about the fatherland, and there would be an acknowledgment that the land is Father's land. Such an acknowledgment in practice would remove one of the principle causes of war. The land of Canaan belonged to God and, as owner, may dispose of his own land as seemeth good in his sight.

2. God gave the land to the children of Israel.

   The Canaanites were usurpers, intruders, squatters. Palestine did not belong to them. They did not have any title deed to the land. The land belonged to God, and God gave it to Israel.

3. The Canaanites were a wicked people.

   Diseased in body, corrupt in mind, sinful in

heart, vile in practice, and abominable in life, character, and conduct, the Canaanites were a menace to mankind.

4. They made the first attack.

   The Canaanites were the aggressors. They began the war. Enemies of God and despisers of God's people, they attacked Israel before Israel attacked them.

5. Their cup of iniquity was full.

   For four centuries God was patient with them. Having crossed the line by us unseen, beyond which there is no hope, and the longsuffering of God having failed to bring them to repentance, there was only one thing left—that one thing was judgment.

   "There is a time we know not when, a place we know not where, that marks the destiny of men, for glory or despair. There is a line by us unseen, that crosses every path, the hidden boundary between God's mercy and His wrath."

6. Nations must be judged as nations.

   There is a judgment for nations as well as for individuals. National sins are followed by national calamity. Since nations do not have a future in another world, they must be judged in this world. The sins of the Canaanites had reached the limit; their cup was full, and as Egypt, Assyria, Babylon, Greece, and Rome, as well as other nations of antiquity were brought to judgment and ruin, so the Canaanites were brought to account, the bill presented and judgment enforced.

7. It became a question of Canaanites or Christ.

(Either the Canaanites must die or Christ could not come.) As certain as Cain murdered Abel, and Isaac would have been slain by Ishmael had God not interfered, as certain as Esau would have corrupted, if not killed, the children of Israel, had God not permitted their extermination. Either Herod must die or Christ must die. Either the Canaanites must perish and Christ live, or the Canaanites live and Christ not be born. Since God is running a universe and not a peanut stand the decision was given in favor of Israel, and the Canaanites must perish. Surgery may not be a pleasant performance, but it may sometimes be necessary to save life. When a tenant (1) fails to pay rent, (2) destroys the property, (3) scandalizes the landlord, (4) kills the children of the landlord, (5) beats the landlord's friends, and (6) corrupts the neighborhood, then the landlord may be justified in ejecting without mercy such a wicked, thankless tenant. Steeped in sin and swept by spiritism, it became necessary to use the surgeon's scissors in order to cut away the sickening cancerous sore. Thus the righteousness of God was vindicated in the rejection and eviction of the Canaanites.

The first thing to remember in connection with the destruction of the Canaanites is that the land of Israel belonged to God. God has a perfect right to do what he wills with his own. God gave the land of Israel to the children of Israel. Abraham occupied the land, Isaac and Jacob were born in the land. The Canaanites were intruders and usurpers, and the land did not belong to them, for the land first belonged to God. He willed it to the children of Israel.

The second thing to remember in considering the destruction of the Canaanites is that the Canaanites were vile born. They were wicked in the extreme. They were not only corrupt and diseased physically but they were rotten mentally, morally, and physically. They were a menace to mankind. They were a liability to humanity.

The third thing to remember in considering the destruction of the Canaanites is that they themselves made the first attack. Israel was acting on the defensive at first. It was not until later that they were ordered to an aggressive warfare in the extermination of the wicked Canaanites.

The fourth thing to remember is that their cup of iniquity was full. They had trifled with God, tampered with the Word of God and tinkered with conscience. The Amorites had been given 400 years grace, for judgment is God's strange work. It is not God's will that any should perish and none are forsaken until their cup of iniquity is full. But, when full, God finally swept them from the earth, using Israel as his besom of destruction.

We need to be reminded that there is a judgment for nations as well as for individuals. Individuals may be judged after death, but nations must be judged while they are yet living nations. God's judgments are always just. His ways are always righteous and in sweeping the Canaanites from the earth it was a distinct act of judgment against them but an act of mercy toward the rest of mankind. In the last analysis it was a question of Christ or no Christ. Either Israel must die or the Canaanites must die. Either the Canaanites must perish or the Israelites must perish, for they could not live together. If Israel died there could be no Calvary, for there would be no Christ. Without Christ there would be neither a Calvary nor a Resurrection. Without Calvary there could be no Pentecost. Without Calvary and Pentecost there could be no redemption. Without redemption, the Bible, and Christ, there could be no salvation. There would never have been a British nation or a United States of America if the Canaanites and other wicked nations had been allowed to live. God in judgment swept them away and, in mercy towards the rest of mankind, made Calvary possible. God is not only dealing with individuals, God is acting with a view to humanity. He has dealt in judgment and mercy with individuals and nations but always and ever with the whole of the race in view.

Canaan belonged to God. God gave it to Israel. The Canaanites were usurpers and intruders. They were not only usurpers and intruders, but were exceeding vile. Their cup of iniquity was filled and judgment was sent. Utter extermination was the only remedy. Christ must be born, if crepe must be hung on the door knob of a nation like Egypt. Christ must be born even though Pharaoh must be wrapped in a winding, watery shroud. Christ must be born if the Hittites and Canaanites all be exterminated, root, branch, and vine, men, women, and children. God is dealing with the race and judgment must follow in the case of individuals as well as of nations, and in nations as well as of individuals. God's ways are right. His works are perfect. His will shall be done in earth as it is done in heaven.

31

CITIES OF REFUGE

(Numbers 35)

1. Kadesh

   The word Kadesh means "holiness" and speaks of Christ as an *holy* refuge.

2. Shechem

   This sets forth Christ as our *Strong Refuge,* for the word Shechem means "shoulder" and speaks of strength to bear, strength to carry. Christ is the strong One, who is able to bear our loads and carry our burdens.

3. Kirjath-arba

   "Fellowship," "communion," "friendship" is the idea conveyed by this word. Not only is Christ an holy refuge and a strong refuge but he is also the one through whom we have communion and fellowship with God.

4. Bezer

   Bezer means "stronghold" and typified Christ as a secure refuge. There is such a thing as security. There is such a thing as eternal security. "My sheep (born again ones) *hear* my voice, and *they follow* me, and I give unto *them* (those who are born again and hear his voice and follow him) eternal life, and they (sheep, hearing—and following) shall never perish." Here is the doctrine of eternal security. Sheep . . . . born again . . . . hearing, listening to God . . . . and following, i.e. obeying.

5. Ramoth

   Ramoth means "to exalt" and speaks of Christ as our high refuge. He has been exalted high above all principalities and powers and now liveth to make intercession for the saints. He came *down* to the deepest depths of humiliation and shame and is exalted to the highest heights of holiness and glory. He is our holy, strong, secure, and high refuge.

6. Golan

   This word means "to exult." As Ramoth speaks of exaltation so Golan speaks of exultation. Conqueror of sin, Satan, death, the grave, and hell, He has not only been exalted but He is also exultant. He is now the glad, joyful, exultant conqueror of all the forces of evil, sin, and wickedness of every kind.

He has triumphed over all the powers of death and darkness, and it is our happy privilege to triumph because of him.

Inside these cities of refuge there was safety, certainty, and enjoyment, while outside there was despair, death, and doom. The manslayer must put forth all his energy to reach the city of refuge. To delay was dangerous and disastrous. To argue or debate meant death. To hesitate would render his escape hopeless. To fight back or fuss would be foolish. He must flee for his life. These cities were easily seen because they were built on a hill, which reminds us that we have a refuge on a hill far away where stood an old rugged cross, the emblem of suffering and shame. The gates were always open, and finger pointers showed the way to the nearest refuge. Thank God for every faithful messenger of the Cross, pointing the way to our holy, strong, secure refuge, even Jesus Christ, God's provision for the failure of man.

32

ZEALOUS DAUGHTERS OF ZELOPHEHAD

(Numbers 36:1-10)

Zelophehad had no part in the crime and rebellion of Korah. He lived and died in the usual way, a hero unheralded, and a saint unsung. He departed this life leaving behind to mourn his loss five dutiful, loving and lovable daughters. These God-fearing girls desired an inheritance in Canaan, the land flowing with milk and honey. All good women may now claim their inheritance in the land. God will answer the prayers and heart cries of all godly girls and women. They may put in their own claim for their own portion. All women everywhere should bless God, honor and love Christ, and seek to be filled with the Holy Spirit, for there is not a square mile of land anywhere on earth where girls and women are respected as they ought to be except where Christ is known and the Bible is preached. The Bible does more to bless women than all other books in all the world put together. The daughters of Zelophehad were also orphans without earthly parents, brothers or protectors. The God of the Bible became a Father, Brother, and Friend.

History is replete with shining examples of

noble women and queenly wives. Words fail to express the profound thankfulness of the soul for sweet girlhood and holy womanhood. In almost every town and city, county and community, there are yet to be found a few godly girls and worshipful women, fit company for the angels in heaven. In this world of woe, sin, and shame, of cruelty and crime, there are nevertheless many matchless Marys kneeling at the Master's feet. In this poor, old, broken-hearted world there are yet to be found godly and loving grandmothers like the grandmother of Timothy. Bending over wornout and tear-stained Bibles, they feed on heavenly manna and teach their sons and grandsons the ways of God. The daughters of Zelophehad loved God and sincerely desired to possess their possessions and enjoy their inheritance in the land of Canaan. They were girls and women that prized purity and holiness above the pleasures of the world. They were women who found their satisfaction in God's will, and their names are recorded in the Book of Life forever.

"I marvel how a woman, with her need of love, with her sensitive, yearning, clasping nature, can look into the face of the Lord Jesus, and not put her arms about his neck, and tell him with gushing love, that she commits herself, body and soul, into his sacred keeping."—Beecher

"Women are the poetry of the world in the same sense as the stars are the poetry of heaven. Clear, light-giving, harmonious, they are the terrestrial planets that rule the destinies of mankind."—Hargrave

"There is one in the world who feels for him who is sad a keener pang than he feels for himself; there is one to whom reflected joy is better than that which comes direct; there is one who rejoices in another's honor more than in any which is one's own; there is one on whom another's transcendent excellence sheds no beam but that of delight; there is one who hides another's infirmities more faithfully than one's own; there is one who loses all sense of *self* in the sentiment of kindness, tenderness, and devotion to another,—that one is WOMAN."—Washington Irving.

33

CHRIST IN THE BOOK OF NUMBERS

All books of the Bible are Christo-centric. The book of Genesis fairly bristles with types and shadows of Christ.

Adam the first, sinless and ruling over a sinless creation, foreshadows the second Man and last Adam, our Lord Jesus Christ.

Abel the suffering, persecuted, and slain shepherd, beautifully sets forth the good, great and chief Shepherd.

Abel's lamb, Isaac's ram, Abraham's heifer, as well as Isaac and Joseph, all typify Christ in his various offices and work.

The book of Exodus is Christo-centric. Moses was born of humble parents and a member of an oppressed race. He lived in a palace but gave up all to suffer with the people of God. A prophet, priest, and king, he married a Gentile bride and now is in heaven. He is a remarkable fore-shadowing of our Lord Jesus Christ. The blood of the Passover lamb, like the lamb itself, was a fore-shadowing of the Lamb of God and the shed blood of Calvary. Like the coats of skins, Abel's lamb, and Isaac's ram, the Passover sets forth our Lord Jesus Christ as the Lamb of God "who taketh away the sin of the world."

As Egypt was a type of the world condemned and ripened for judgment, and as Moses delivered Israel from Egypt, and as they were delivered through the shedding of innocent blood, so Christ and his shed blood delivers us from this condemned and evil world now ripening for judgment. As Pharaoh was a type of the devil who with his wiles and enmity oppressed the Children of Israel, so Christ delivers his people from the wiles of the Devil. The Passover Lamb, without blemish, slain, its blood shed, and its blood sprinkled, although not a bone of it was broken, all sets forth our Lord Jesus Christ as the spotless Lamb of God.

The smitten rock pointed forward to the Rock of Ages whose side would be smitten, and from that wounded side there would flow a stream of living water and cleansing blood. The pillar of the cloud by day and the fire by night was a great symbol of the presence of God with his people, guiding, sheltering, alike by day and by night. The manna, which came down from heaven, was white, round, sweet, nourishing, and for the most part passed away unheaded, was only one more great foreshadowing of the Bread of God, the Bread of angels and the Bread of Life who came down from heaven.

The tabernacle also points to Christ. The materials which were gold, silver, brass, blue, purple, scarlet, fine linen, all set forth our Lord Jesus Christ as the divine redeemer, righteous, heavenly, royal, suffering, spotless Son of man and Son of

God. The furniture of the tabernacle sets forth the presence of Christ with us even to the end of the age. The mercy seat points to Christ on high as our mercy seat. The golden altar of incense points to Jesus Christ's ascension now to the right hand of the majesty of heaven. The candlestick prefigures Christ as the Light of the world. Thus the materials by which the tabernacle was made, and the furniture within its sacred precincts, all set forth Christ as the glorious Son of God. The book of Genesis is Christo-centric. The book of Exodus is also Christo-centric.

The book of Leviticus is also Christo-centric. The problem of Leviticus is, How can sinful man approach a holy God? This problem is met by the offerings such as a bullock which sets forth Christ as the servant of God and man, a lamb or goat which sets forth Christ as the Lamb of God and the One who was made a curse for us. The turtle dove or pigeons set forth Christ as the heavenly One come down to earth to suffer and die. The meal offering sets forth Christ as the Bread of Life, together with the peace offering which pre-figures Christ as having made peace by the blood of his cross, the sin offering and the trespass offering all making provision for some great need of man. Christ is our trespass offering. Christ is our sin offering and Christ is our meal offering. Christ is our peace offering. Christ is our burnt offering.

Aaron, the High priest sets forth Jesus Christ

as our high priest now interceding for us. The two birds by which the leper was cleansed sets forth Jesus Christ as having died and risen again. The dead bird preaches that Christ died for us. The living bird preaches that Christ rose again, ascended on high and became the justifier of all who believe. Christ is thus set forth in Leviticus was well as Exodus and Genesis. The two goats on the great day of atonement show the Christ who was made a curse for us. The dead goat tells that Christ died for our sins. The live goat declares that Christ arose again and carries our sins into the land of forgetfulness to be remembered no more against us forever.

The feasts of Israel set forth Christ as our Passover, Christ as our Pentecostal purifier, Christ as our coming King. Thus Christ is all in all. The old Testament, like the New Testament, is Christocentric.

34

BOOK OF NUMBERS IS CHRISTO-CENTRIC

1. Moses
   Type of Christ as prophet, priest and king
2. Aaron
   Type of Christ as our High Priest
3. Passover
   Type of Christ on the Cross
4. The red heifer
   Type of Christ as the suffering servant of God and of man
5. The brazen serpent
   Type of Christ as the one who became a curse for us
6. The smitten rock
   Type of Christ as the sure and certain foundation for all our peace and hope.
7. The cities of refuge
   Type of Christ as our shelter and protection from the onslaughts of Satan and sin
8. The candlestick
   Type of Christ as the Light of the World.

9. The Nazarite

   Type of Christ as the separated one, holy, harmless, and undefiled

10. The Star of Jacob

    Type of Christ as the glory of Israel as well as the Light to enlighten the Gentiles

11. The Bread of Life (11:7-9)

12. The Water of Life (20:11)

"Are you willing to be a highway over which Jesus Christ shall come to your town and into the lives of your friends and neighbors? Right of way costs something. When President Garfield was shot, he was taken to a quiet, isolated house where he could have absolute quiet and rest in his fight for life, and a special railway was constructed to facilitate the bringing of doctors, nurses, and loved ones to his bedside. The engineers laid out the line to cross a farmer's front yard, but he refused to grant the right of way until they explained to him that it was for the President, when he exclaimed, 'That is different. Why, if that railroad is for the President, you can run it right through my house.' Are you willing to give Him right of way across your front yard? It may run right through some of your plans, or social engagements, or business appointments. But will you give him the right of way?"—Michigan Christian Advocate

"But here was One,
Faultless though compassed with infirmity,
In human weakness sinless, who had stooped
Lower than angelhood in might, but dwarfed
In uncreated goodness infinite.
The loftiest seraphim. No stern recluse,
As his forerunner; but the guest and friend,
Of all who sought Him, mingling with all life
To breathe His holiness on all. No film
Obscured his spotless lustre. From His life
Truth limpid without error flow'd. Disease
Fled from His touch. Pain heard Him, and was not.
Despair smiled in His presence. Devils knew,
And trembled. In the omnipotence of faith
Unintermittent, indefectible.
Leaning upon His Father's might, He bent
All nature to His will. The tempest sank,
He whispering, into waveless calm. The bread,
Given from his hands, fed thousands and to spare.
The stormy waters, or the solid rock,
Were payment for His footsteps. Death itself,
With vain reluctance yielded its prey
To the stern mandate of the Prince of Life."

—Bickersteth